THE YEAR OF
MAGICAL THINKING

Also by Joan Didion

THE YEAR OF
MAGICAL
THINKING

JOAN DIDION

FOURTH ESTATE · *London*

First published in Great Britain in 2005 by

Fourth Estate

An imprint of HarperCollins*Publishers*

77–85 Fulham Palace Road

London W6 8JB

www.4thestate.co.uk

4

A catalogue record for this book is
available from the British Library

ISBN-13 978-0-00-721684-0

ISBN-10 0-00-721684-X

Printed in Great Britain by Clays Ltd, St Ives plc

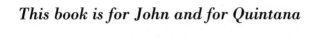

This book is for John and for Quintana

THE YEAR OF
MAGICAL
THINKING

1.

Life changes fast.
Life changes in the instant.
You sit down to dinner and life as you know it ends.
The question of self-pity.

Those were the first words I wrote after it happened. The computer dating on the Microsoft Word file ("Notes on change.doc") reads "May 20, 2004, 11:11 p.m.," but that would have been a case of my opening the file and reflexively pressing save when I closed it. I had made no changes to that file in May. I had made no changes to that file since I wrote the words, in January 2004, a day or two or three after the fact.

For a long time I wrote nothing else.

Life changes in the instant.

The ordinary instant.

At some point, in the interest of remembering what

seemed most striking about what had happened, I considered adding those words, "the ordinary instant." I saw
immediately that there would be no need to add the word
"ordinary," because there would be no forgetting it: the
word never left my mind. It was in fact the ordinary nature
of everything preceding the event that prevented me from
truly believing it had happened, absorbing it, incorporat-
ing it, getting past it. I recognize now that there was nothing unusual in this: confronted with sudden disaster we
all focus on how unremarkable the circumstances were
in which the unthinkable occurred, the clear blue sky
from which the plane fell, the routine errand that ended
on the shoulder with the car in flames, the swings where
the children were playing as usual when the rattlesnake
struck from the ivy. "He was on his way home from
work—happy, successful, healthy—and then, gone," I
read in the account of a psychiatric nurse whose husband
was killed in a highway accident. In 1966 I happened to
interview many people who had been living in Honolulu
on the morning of December 7, 1941; without exception,
these people began their accounts of Pearl Harbor by
telling me what an "ordinary Sunday morning" it had
been. "It was just an ordinary beautiful September day,"
people still say when asked to describe the morning in
New York when American Airlines 11 and United
Airlines 175 got flown into the World Trade towers. Even
the report of the 9/11 Commission opened on this insis-

tently premonitory and yet still dumbstruck narrative note: "Tuesday, September 11, 2001, dawned temperate and nearly cloudless in the eastern United States."

"And then—gone." *In the midst of life we are in death,* Episcopalians say at the graveside. Later I realized that I must have repeated the details of what happened to everyone who came to the house in those first weeks, all those friends and relatives who brought food and made drinks and laid out plates on the dining room table for however many people were around at lunch or dinner time, all those who picked up the plates and froze the leftovers and ran the dishwasher and filled our (I could not yet think *my*) otherwise empty house even after I had gone into the bedroom (our bedroom, the one in which there still lay on a sofa a faded terrycloth XL robe bought in the 1970s at Richard Carroll in Beverly Hills) and shut the door. Those moments when I was abruptly overtaken by exhaustion are what I remember most clearly about the first days and weeks. I have no memory of telling anyone the details, but I must have done so, because everyone seemed to know them. At one point I considered the possibility that they had picked up the details of the story from one another, but immediately rejected it: the story they had was in each instance too accurate to have been passed from hand to hand. It had come from me.

Another reason I knew that the story had come from

me was that no version I heard included the details I could not yet face, for example the blood on the living room floor that stayed there until José came in the next morning and cleaned it up.

José. Who was part of our household. Who was supposed to be flying to Las Vegas later that day, December 31, but never went. José was crying that morning as he cleaned up the blood. When I first told him what had happened he had not understood. Clearly I was not the ideal teller of this story, something about my version had been at once too offhand and too elliptical, something in my tone had failed to convey the central fact in the situation (I would encounter the same failure later when I had to tell Quintana), but by the time José saw the blood he understood.

I had picked up the abandoned syringes and ECG electrodes before he came in that morning but I could not face the blood.

In outline.

It is now, as I begin to write this, the afternoon of October 4, 2004.

Nine months and five days ago, at approximately nine o'clock on the evening of December 30, 2003, my hus-

band, John Gregory Dunne, appeared to (or did) experience, at the table where he and I had just sat down to
dinner in the living room of our apartment in New York, a
sudden massive coronary event that caused his death.
Our only child, Quintana, had been for the previous five
nights unconscious in an intensive care unit at Beth
Israel Medical Center's Singer Division, at that time a
hospital on East End Avenue (it closed in August 2004)
more commonly known as "Beth Israel North" or "the old
Doctors' Hospital," where what had seemed a case of
December flu sufficiently severe to take her to an emergency room on Christmas morning had exploded into
pneumonia and septic shock. This is my attempt to make
sense of the period that followed, weeks and then months
that cut loose any fixed idea I had ever had about death,
about illness, about probability and luck, about good for-
tune and bad, about marriage and children and memory,
about grief, about the ways in which people do and do not
deal with the fact that life ends, about the shallowness of
sanity, about life itself. I have been a writer my entire
life. As a writer, even as a child, long before what I wrote
began to be published, I developed a sense that meaning
itself was resident in the rhythms of words and sentences
and paragraphs, a technique for withholding whatever it
was I thought or believed behind an increasingly impenetrable polish. The way I write is who I am, or have become, yet this is a case in which I wish I had instead of

words and their rhythms a cutting room, equipped with an Avid, a digital editing system on which I could touch a key and collapse the sequence of time, show you simultaneously all the frames of memory that come to me now, let you pick the takes, the marginally different expressions, the variant readings of the same lines. This is a case in which I need more than words to find the meaning. This is a case in which I need whatever it is I think or believe to be penetrable, if only for myself.

2.

December 30, 2003, a Tuesday.
    We had seen Quintana in the sixth-floor ICU at Beth Israel North.

We had come home.

We had discussed whether to go out for dinner or eat in.

I said I would build a fire, we could eat in.

I built the fire, I started dinner, I asked John if he wanted a drink.

I got him a Scotch and gave it to him in the living room, where he was reading in the chair by the fire where he habitually sat.

The book he was reading was by David Fromkin, a bound galley of *Europe's Last Summer: Who Started the Great War in 1914?*

I finished getting dinner, I set the table in the living room where, when we were home alone, we could eat within sight of the fire. I find myself stressing the fire be-

cause fires were important to us. I grew up in California,
John and I lived there together for twenty-four years, in
California we heated our houses by building fires. We
built fires even on summer evenings, because the fog
came in. Fires said we were home, we had drawn the cir-
cle, we were safe through the night. I lit the candles. John
asked for a second drink before sitting down. I gave it to
him. We sat down. My attention was on mixing the salad.

John was talking, then he wasn't.

At one point in the seconds or minute before he
stopped talking he had asked me if I had used single-
malt Scotch for his second drink. I had said no, I used the
same Scotch I had used for his first drink. "Good," he
had said. "I don't know why but I don't think you should
mix them." At another point in those seconds or that
minute he had been talking about why World War One
was the critical event from which the entire rest of the
twentieth century flowed.

I have no idea which subject we were on, the Scotch or
World War One, at the instant he stopped talking.

I only remember looking up. His left hand was raised
and he was slumped motionless. At first I thought he was
making a failed joke, an attempt to make the difficulty of
the day seem manageable.

I remember saying *Don't do that.*

When he did not respond my first thought was that he
had started to eat and choked. I remember trying to lift

him far enough from the back of the chair to give him the Heimlich. I remember the sense of his weight as he fell forward, first against the table, then to the floor. In the kitchen by the telephone I had taped a card with the New York–Presbyterian ambulance numbers. I had not taped the numbers by the telephone because I anticipated a moment like this. I had taped the numbers by the telephone in case someone in the building needed an ambulance.

Someone else.

I called one of the numbers. A dispatcher asked if he was breathing. I said *Just come.* When the paramedics came I tried to tell them what had happened but before I could finish they had transformed the part of the living room where John lay into an emergency department. One of them (there were three, maybe four, even an hour later I could not have said) was talking to the hospital about the electrocardiogram they seemed already to be transmitting. Another was opening the first or second of what would be many syringes for injection. (Epinephrine? Lidocaine? Procainamide? The names came to mind but I had no idea from where.) I remember saying that he might have choked. This was dismissed with a finger swipe: the airway was clear. They seemed now to be using defibrillating paddles, an attempt to restore a rhythm. They got something that could have been a normal heartbeat (or I thought they did, we had all been silent, there was a sharp jump), then lost it, and started again.

"He's still fibbing," I remember the one on the telephone saying.

"*V*-fibbing," John's cardiologist said the next morning when he called from Nantucket. "They would have said '*V*-fibbing.' V for ventricular."

Maybe they said "V-fibbing" and maybe they did not. Atrial fibrillation did not immediately or necessarily cause cardiac arrest. Ventricular did. Maybe ventricular was the given.

I remember trying to straighten out in my mind what would happen next. Since there was an ambulance crew in the living room, the next logical step would be going to the hospital. It occurred to me that the crew could decide very suddenly to go to the hospital and I would not be ready. I would not have in hand what I needed to take. I would waste time, get left behind. I found my handbag and a set of keys and a summary John's doctor had made of his medical history. When I got back to the living room the paramedics were watching the computer monitor they had set up on the floor. I could not see the monitor so I watched their faces. I remember one glancing at the others. When the decision was made to move it happened very fast. I followed them to the elevator and asked if I could go with them. They said they were taking the gurney down first, I could go in the second ambulance. One of them waited with me for the elevator to come back up. By the time he and I got into the second ambulance the ambulance carrying the gurney was pulling away from the front of the building. The distance from our building to the part of New York–Presbyterian that used to be New York Hospital is six crosstown blocks. I have no memory of sirens. I have no memory of traffic. When we arrived at the emergency entrance to the hospital the gurney was already disappearing into the building. A man was waiting in the driveway. Everyone else in sight was wearing scrubs. He was not. "Is this the wife," he said to the driver, then turned to me. "I'm your social worker," he said, and I guess that is when I must have known.

"I opened the door and I seen the man in the dress greens and I knew. I immediately knew." This was what the mother of a nineteen-year-old killed by a bomb in Kirkuk said on an HBO documentary quoted by Bob Herbert in *The New York Times* on the morning of November 12, 2004. "But I thought that if, as long as I didn't let him in, he couldn't tell me. And then it—none of that would've happened. So he kept saying, 'Ma'am, I need to come in.' And I kept telling him, 'I'm sorry, but you can't come in.' "

When I read this at breakfast almost eleven months after the night with the ambulance and the social worker I recognized the thinking as my own.

Inside the emergency room I could see the gurney being pushed into a cubicle, propelled by more people in scrubs. Someone told me to wait in the reception area. I did. There was a line for admittance paperwork. Waiting in the line seemed the constructive thing to do. Waiting in the line said that there was still time to deal with this, I had copies of the insurance cards in my handbag, this was not a hospital I had ever negotiated—New York Hospital was the Cornell part of New York–Presbyterian, the part I knew was the Columbia part, Columbia-Presbyterian, at 168th and Broadway, twenty minutes away at best, too far in this kind of emergency—but I could make this unfamiliar hospital work, I could be useful, I could arrange the transfer to Columbia-Presbyterian once he was stabilized. I was fixed on the details of this imminent transfer to Columbia (he would need a bed with telemetry, eventually I could also get Quintana transferred to Columbia, the night she was admitted to Beth Israel North I had written on a card the beeper numbers of several Columbia doctors, one or another of them could make all this happen) when the social worker reappeared and guided me from the paperwork line into an empty room off the reception area. "You can wait here," he said. I waited. The room was cold, or I was.

I wondered how much time had passed between the time I called the ambulance and the arrival of the paramedics. It had seemed no time at all (*a mote in the eye of God* was the phrase that came to me in the room off the reception area) but it must have been at the minimum several minutes.

I used to have on a bulletin board in my office, for reasons having to do with a plot point in a movie, a pink index card on which I had typed a sentence from *The Merck Manual* about how long the brain can be deprived of oxygen. The image of the pink index card was coming back to me in the room off the reception area: "Tissue anoxia for > 4 to 6 min. can result in irreversible brain damage or death." I was telling myself that I must be misremembering the sentence when the social worker reappeared. He had with him a man he introduced as "your husband's doctor." There was a silence. "He's dead, isn't he," I heard myself say to the doctor. The doctor looked at the social worker. "It's okay," the social worker said. "She's a pretty cool customer." They took me into the curtained cubicle where John lay, alone now. They asked if I wanted a priest. I said yes. A priest appeared and said the words. I thanked him. They gave me the silver clip in which John kept his driver's license and credit cards. They gave me the cash that had been in his pocket. They gave me his watch. They gave me his cell phone. They gave me a plastic bag in which they said I would find his clothes. I thanked them. The social worker asked if he could do anything more for me. I said he could put me in a taxi. He did. I thanked him. "Do you have money for the fare," he asked. I said I did, the cool customer. When I walked into the apartment and saw John's jacket and scarf still lying on the chair where he had dropped them when we came in from seeing Quintana at Beth Israel North (the red cashmere scarf, the Patagonia windbreaker that had been the crew jacket on *Up Close & Personal*) I wondered what an uncool customer would be allowed to do. Break down? Require sedation? Scream?

I remember thinking that I needed to discuss this with John.

There was nothing I did not discuss with John.

Because we were both writers and both worked at home our days were filled with the sound of each other's voices.

I did not always think he was right nor did he always think I was right but we were each the person the other trusted. There was no separation between our investments or interests in any given situation. Many people assumed that we must be, since sometimes one and sometimes the other would get the better review, the bigger advance, in some way "competitive," that our private life must be a minefield of professional envies and resentments. This was so far from the case that the general insistence on it came to suggest certain lacunae in the popular understanding of marriage.

That had been one more thing we discussed.

What I remember about the apartment the night I came home alone from New York Hospital was its silence.

In the plastic bag I had been given at the hospital there were a pair of corduroy pants, a wool shirt, a belt, and I think nothing else. The legs of the corduroy pants had been slit open, I supposed by the paramedics. There was blood on the shirt. The belt was braided. I remember putting his cell phone in the charger on his desk. I remember putting his silver clip in the box in the bedroom in which we kept passports and birth certificates and proof of jury service. I look now at the clip and see that these were the cards he was carrying: a New York State driver's license, due for renewal on May 25, 2004; a Chase ATM card; an American Express card; a Wells Fargo MasterCard; a Metropolitan Museum card; a Writers Guild of America West card (it was the season before Academy voting, when you could use a WGAW card to see movies free, he must have gone to a movie, I did not remember); a Medicare card; a Metro card; and a card issued by Medtronic with the legend "I have a Kappa 900 SR pacemaker implanted," the serial number of the device, a number to call for the doctor who implanted it, and the notation "Implant Date: 03 Jun 2003." I remember combining the cash that had been in his pocket with the cash in my own bag, smoothing the bills, taking special care to interleaf twenties with twenties, tens with tens, fives and ones with fives and ones. I remember thinking as I did this that he would see that I was handling things.

When I saw him in the curtained cubicle in the emergency room at New York Hospital there was a chip in one of his front teeth, I supposed from the fall, since there were also bruises on his face. When I identified his body the next day at Frank E. Campbell the bruises were not apparent. It occurred to me that masking the bruises must have been what the undertaker meant when I said no embalming and he said "in that case we'll just clean him up." The part with the undertaker remains remote. I had arrived at Frank E. Campbell so determined to avoid any inappropriate response (tears, anger, helpless laughter at the Oz-like hush) that I had shut down all response. After my mother died the undertaker who picked up her body left in its place on the bed an artificial rose. My brother had told me this, offended to the core. I would be armed against artificial roses. I remember making a brisk decision about a coffin. I remember that in the office where I signed the papers there was a grandfather's clock, not running. John's nephew Tony Dunne, who was with me, mentioned to the undertaker that the clock was not running. The undertaker, as if pleased to elucidate a decorative element, explained that the clock had not run in some years, but was retained as "a kind of memorial" to a previous incarnation of the firm. He seemed to be offering the clock as a lesson. I concentrated on Quintana. I could shut out what the undertaker was saying but I could not shut out the lines I was hearing as I concentrated on Quintana: *Full fathom five thy father lies / Those are pearls that were his eyes.*

Eight months later I asked the manager of our apartment building if he still had the log kept by the doormen for the night of December 30. I knew there was a log, I had been for three years president of the board of the building, the door log was intrinsic to building procedure. The next day the manager sent me the page for December 30. According to the log the doormen that night were Michael Flynn and Vasile Ionescu. I had not remembered that. Vasile Ionescu and John had a routine with which they amused themselves in the elevator, a small game, between an exile from Ceauşescu's Romania and an Irish Catholic from West Hartford, Connecticut, based on a shared appreciation of political posturing. "So where is bin Laden," Vasile would say when John got onto the elevator, the point being to come up with ever more improbable suggestions: "Could bin Laden be in the penthouse?" "In the maisonette?" "In the fitness room?" When I saw Vasile's name on the log it occurred to me that I could not remember if he had initiated this game when we came in from Beth Israel North in the early evening of December 30. The log for that evening showed only two entries, fewer than usual, even for a time of the year when most people in the building left for more clement venues:

> NOTE: Paramedics arrived at 9:20 p.m. for
> Mr. Dunne. Mr. Dunne was taken to
> hospital at 10:05 p.m.
> NOTE: Lightbulb out on A-B passenger
> elevator.

The A-B elevator was our elevator, the elevator on which the paramedics came up at 9:20 p.m., the elevator on which they took John (and me) downstairs to the ambulance at 10:05 p.m., the elevator on which I returned alone to our apartment at a time not noted. I had not noticed a lightbulb being out on the elevator. Nor had

I noticed that the paramedics were in the apartment for forty-five minutes. I had always described it as "fifteen or twenty minutes." *If they were here that long does it mean that he was alive?* I put this question to a doctor I knew. "Sometimes they'll work that long," he said. It was a while before I realized that this in no way addressed the question.

The death certificate, when I got it, gave the time of death as 10:18 p.m., December 30, 2003.

I had been asked before I left the hospital if I would authorize an autopsy. I had said yes. I later read that asking a survivor to authorize an autopsy is seen in hospitals as delicate, sensitive, often the most difficult of the routine steps that follow a death. Doctors themselves, according to many studies (for example Katz, J. L., and Gardner, R., "The Intern's Dilemma: The Request for Autopsy Consent," *Psychiatry in Medicine* 3:197–203, 1972), experience considerable anxiety about making the request. They know that autopsy is essential to the learning and teaching of medicine, but they also know that the procedure touches a primitive dread. If whoever it was at New York Hospital who asked me to authorize an autopsy experienced such anxiety I could have spared

him or her: I actively wanted an autopsy. I actively
wanted an autopsy even though I had seen some, in the
course of doing research. I knew exactly what occurs, the
chest open like a chicken in a butcher's case, the face
peeled down, the scale in which the organs are weighed.
I had seen homicide detectives avert their eyes from an
autopsy in progress. I still wanted one. I needed to know
how and why and when it had happened. In fact I wanted
to be in the room when they did it (I had watched those
other autopsies with John, I owed him his own, it was
fixed in my mind at that moment that he would be in the
room if I were on the table) but I did not trust myself to rationally present the point so I did not ask.

If the ambulance left our building at 10:05 p.m., and
death was declared at 10:18 p.m., the thirteen minutes in
between were just bookkeeping, bureaucracy, making
sure the hospital procedures were observed and the paperwork was done and the appropriate person was on
hand to do the sign-off, inform the cool customer.

The sign-off, I later learned, was called the "pro-
nouncement," as in "Pronounced: 10:18 p.m."

I had to believe he was dead all along.

If I did not believe he was dead all along I would have
thought I should have been able to save him.

Until I saw the autopsy report I continued to think this
anyway, an example of delusionary thinking, the omnipo-
tent variety.

A week or two before he died, when we were having dinner in a restaurant, John asked me to write something in my notebook for him. He always carried cards on which to make notes, three-by-six-inch cards printed with his name that could be slipped into an inside pocket. At dinner he had thought of something he wanted to remember but when he looked in his pockets he found no cards. I need you to write something down, he said. It was, he said, for his new book, not for mine, a point he stressed because I was at the time researching a book that involved sports. This was the note he dictated: "Coaches used to go out after a game and say 'you played great.' Now they go out with state police, as if this were a war and they the military. The militarization of sports." When I gave him the note the next day he said "You can use it if you want to."

What did he mean?

Did he know he would not write the book?

Did he have some apprehension, a shadow? Why had he forgotten to bring note cards to dinner that night? Had he not warned me when I forgot my own notebook that the ability to make a note when something came to mind was the difference between being able to write and not being able to write? Was something telling him that night that the time for being able to write was running out?

One summer when we were living in Brentwood Park we fell into a pattern of stopping work at four in the afternoon and going out to the pool. He would stand in the water reading (he reread *Sophie's Choice* several times that summer, trying to see how it worked) while I worked in the garden. It was a small, even miniature, garden with gravel paths and a rose arbor and beds edged with thyme and santolina and feverfew. I had convinced John a few years before that we should tear out a lawn to plant this garden. To my surprise, since he had shown no previous interest in gardens, he regarded the finished product as an almost mystical gift. Just before five on those summer afternoons we would swim and then go into the library wrapped in towels to watch *Tenko*, a BBC series, then in syndication, about a number of satisfyingly predictable English women (one was immature and selfish, another seemed to have been written with *Mrs. Miniver* in mind) imprisoned by the Japanese in Malaya during World War Two. After each afternoon's *Tenko* segment we would go upstairs and work another hour or two, John in his office at the top of the stairs, me in the glassed-in porch across the hall that had become my office. At seven or seven-thirty we would go out to dinner, many nights at Morton's. Morton's felt right that summer. There was always shrimp quesadilla, chicken with black beans. There was always someone we knew. The room was cool and polished and dark inside but you could see the twilight outside.

John did not like driving at night by then. This was one reason, I later learned, that he wanted to spend more

time in New York, a wish that at the time remained mysterious to me. One night that summer he asked me to drive
home after dinner at Anthea Sylbert's house on Camino
Palmero in Hollywood. I remember thinking how remarkable this was. Anthea lived less than a block from a house
on Franklin Avenue in which we had lived from 1967
until 1971, so it was not a question of reconnoitering a
new neighborhood. It had occurred to me as I started the
ignition that I could count on my fingers the number of
times I had driven when John was in the car; the single
other time I could remember that night was once spelling
him on a drive from Las Vegas to Los Angeles. He had
been dozing in the passenger seat of the Corvette we then
had. He had opened his eyes. After a moment he had
said, very carefully, "I might take it a little slower." I had
no sense of unusual speed and glanced at the speedome-
ter: I was doing 120.

Yet.

A drive across the Mojave was one thing. There had
been no previous time when he asked me to drive home
from dinner in town: this evening on Camino Palmero
was unprecedented. So was the fact that at the end of the
forty-minute drive to Brentwood Park he pronounced it
"well driven."

He mentioned those afternoons with the pool and the
garden and *Tenko* several times during the year before he
died.

Philippe Ariès, in *The Hour of Our Death*, points out that the essential characteristic of death as it appears in the *Chanson de Roland* is that the death, even if sudden or accidental, "gives advance warning of its arrival." Gawain is asked: "Ah, good my lord, think you then so soon to die?" Gawain answers: "I tell you that I shall not live two days." Ariès notes: "Neither his doctor nor his friends nor the priests (the latter are absent and forgotten) know as much about it as he. Only the dying man can tell how much time he has left."

You sit down to dinner.

"You can use it if you want to," John had said when I gave him the note he had dictated a week or two before.

And then—gone.

Grief, when it comes, is nothing we expect it to be. It was not what I felt when my parents died: my father died a few days short of his eighty-fifth birthday and my mother a month short of her ninety-first, both after some years of increasing debility. What I felt in each instance was sadness, loneliness (the loneliness of the abandoned child of whatever age), regret for time gone by, for things unsaid, for my inability to share or even in any real way to acknowledge, at the end, the pain and helplessness and physical humiliation they each endured. I understood the inevitability of each of their deaths. I had been expecting (fearing, dreading, anticipating) those deaths all my life. They remained, when they did occur, distanced, at a remove from the ongoing dailiness of my life. After my mother died I received a letter from a friend in Chicago, a former Maryknoll priest, who precisely intuited what I felt. The death of a parent, he wrote, "despite our preparation, indeed, despite our age, dislodges things deep in us, sets off reactions that surprise us and that may cut free memories and feelings that we had thought gone to ground long ago. We might, in that indeterminate period they call mourning, be in a submarine, silent on the ocean's bed, aware of the depth charges, now near and now far, buffeting us with recollections."

My father was dead, my mother was dead, I would need for a while to watch for mines, but I would still get up in the morning and send out the laundry.

I would still plan a menu for Easter lunch.

I would still remember to renew my passport.

Grief is different. Grief has no distance. Grief comes in waves, paroxysms, sudden apprehensions that weaken the knees and blind the eyes and obliterate the dailiness of life. Virtually everyone who has ever experienced grief mentions this phenomenon of "waves." Eric Lindemann, who was chief of psychiatry at Massachusetts General Hospital in the 1940s and interviewed many family members of those killed in the 1942 Cocoanut Grove fire, defined the phenomenon with absolute specificity in a famous 1944 study: "sensations of somatic distress occurring in waves lasting from twenty minutes to an hour at a time, a feeling of tightness in the throat, choking with shortness of breath, need for sighing, and an empty feeling in the abdomen, lack of muscular power, and an intense subjective distress described as tension or mental pain."

Tightness in the throat.

Choking, need for sighing.

Such waves began for me on the morning of December 31, 2003, seven or eight hours after the fact, when I woke alone in the apartment. I do not remember crying the night before; I had entered at the moment it happened a kind of shock in which the only thought I allowed myself was that there must be certain things I needed to do. There had been certain things I had needed to do while the ambulance crew was in the living room. I had needed for example to get the copy of John's medical summary, so I could take it with me to the hospital. I had needed for example to bank the fire, because I would be leaving it. There had been certain things I had needed to do at the hospital. I had needed for example to stand in the line. I had needed for example to focus on the bed with telemetry he would need for the transfer to Columbia-Presbyterian.

Once I got back from the hospital there had again been certain things I needed to do. I could not identify all of these things but I did know one of them: I needed, before I did anything else, to tell John's brother Nick. It had seemed too late in the evening to call their older brother Dick on Cape Cod (he went to bed early, his health had not been good, I did not want to wake him with bad news) but I needed to tell Nick. I did not plan how to do this. I just sat on the bed and picked up the phone and dialed the number of his house in Connecticut. He answered. I told him. After I put down the phone, in what I can only describe as a new neural pattern of dialing numbers and saying the words, I picked it up again. I could not call Quintana (she was still where we had left her a few hours before, unconscious in the ICU at Beth Israel North) but I could call Gerry, her husband of five months, and I could call my brother, Jim, who would be at his house in Pebble Beach. Gerry said he would come over. I said there was no need to come over, I would be fine. Jim said he would get a flight. I said there was no need to think about a flight, we would talk in the morning. I was trying to think what to do next when the phone rang. It was John's and my agent, Lynn Nesbit, a friend since I suppose the late sixties. It was not clear to me at the time how she knew but she did (it had something to do with a mutual friend to whom both Nick and Lynn seemed in the last minute to have spoken) and she was calling from

a taxi on her way to our apartment. At one level I was re-
lieved (Lynn knew how to manage things, Lynn would
know what it was that I was supposed to be doing) and at
another I was bewildered: how could I deal at this moment with company? What would we do, would we sit in
the living room with the syringes and the ECG electrodes
and the blood still on the floor, should I rekindle what
was left of the fire, would we have a drink, would she
have eaten?

Had I eaten?

The instant in which I asked myself whether I had
eaten was the first intimation of what was to come: if I
thought of food, I learned that night, I would throw up.

Lynn arrived.

We sat in the part of the living room where the blood
and electrodes and syringes were not.

I remember thinking as I was talking to Lynn (this was
the part I could not say) that the blood must have come
from the fall: he had fallen on his face, there was the
chipped tooth I had noticed in the emergency room, the
tooth could have cut the inside of his mouth.

Lynn picked up the phone and said that she was calling Christopher.

This was another bewilderment: the Christopher I
knew best was Christopher Dickey, but he was in either
Paris or Dubai and in any case Lynn would have said
Chris, not Christopher. I found my mind veering to the

autopsy. It could even be happening as I sat there. Then I realized that the Christopher to whom Lynn was talking was Christopher Lehmann-Haupt, who was the chief obituary writer for *The New York Times*. I remember a sense of shock. I wanted to say *not yet* but my mouth had gone dry. I could deal with "autopsy" but the notion of "obituary" had not occurred to me. "Obituary," unlike "autopsy," which was between me and John and the hospital, meant it had happened. I found myself wondering, with no sense of illogic, if it had also happened in Los Angeles. I was trying to work out what time it had been when he died and whether it was that time yet in Los Angeles. (Was there time to go back? Could we have a different ending on Pacific time?) I recall being seized by a pressing need not to let anyone at the *Los Angeles Times* learn what had happened by reading it in *The New York Times*. I called our closest friend at the *Los Angeles Times*, Tim Rutten. I have no memory of what Lynn and I did then. I remember her saying that she would stay the night, but I said no, I would be fine alone.

And I was.

Until the morning. When, only half awake, I tried to think why I was alone in the bed. There was a leaden feeling. It was the same leaden feeling with which I woke on mornings after John and I had fought. Had we had a fight? What about, how had it started, how could we fix it if I could not remember how it started?

Then I remembered.

For several weeks that would be the way I woke to the day.

I wake and feel the fell of dark, not day.

One of several lines from different poems by Gerard Manley Hopkins that John strung together during the months immediately after his younger brother committed suicide, a kind of improvised rosary.

O the mind, mind has mountains; cliffs of fall
Frightful, sheer, no-man-fathomed. Hold them cheap
May who ne'er hung there.
I wake and feel the fell of dark, not day.
And I have asked to be
Where no storms come.

I see now that my insistence on spending that first night alone was more complicated than it seemed, a primitive instinct. Of course I knew John was dead. Of course I had already delivered the definitive news to his brother and to my brother and to Quintana's husband. *The New York Times* knew. The *Los Angeles Times* knew. Yet I was myself in no way prepared to accept this news as final: there was a level on which I believed that what had happened remained reversible. That was why I needed to be alone.

After that first night I would not be alone for weeks (Jim and his wife Gloria would fly in from California the next day, Nick would come back to town, Tony and his wife Rosemary would come down from Connecticut, José would not go to Las Vegas, our assistant Sharon would come back from skiing, there would never not be people in the house), but I needed that first night to be alone.

I needed to be alone so that he could come back.

This was the beginning of my year of magical thinking.

3.

The power of grief to derange the mind has in fact been exhaustively noted. The act of grieving, Freud told us in his 1917 "Mourning and Melancholia," "involves grave departures from the normal attitude to life." Yet, he pointed out, grief remains peculiar among derangements: "It never occurs to us to regard it as a pathological condition and to refer it to medical treatment." We rely instead on "its being overcome after a certain lapse of time." We view "any interference with it as useless and even harmful." Melanie Klein, in her 1940 "Mourning and Its Relation to Manic-Depressive States," made a similar assessment: "The mourner is in fact ill, but because this state of mind is common and seems so natural to us, we do not call mourning an illness. . . . To put my conclusion more precisely: I should say that in mourning the subject goes through a modified and transitory manic-depressive state and overcomes it."

Notice the stress on "overcoming" it.

It was deep into the summer, some months after the night when I needed to be alone so that he could come back, before I recognized that through the winter and spring there had been occasions on which I was incapable of thinking rationally. I was thinking as small children think, as if my thoughts or wishes had the power to reverse the narrative, change the outcome. In my case this disordered thinking had been covert, noticed I think by no one else, hidden even from me, but it had also been, in retrospect, both urgent and constant. In retrospect there had been signs, warning flags I should have noticed. There had been for example the matter of the obituaries. I could not read them. This continued from December 31, when the first obituaries appeared, until February 29, the night of the 2004 Academy Awards, when I saw a photograph of John in the Academy's "In Memoriam" montage. When I saw the photograph I realized for the first time why the obituaries had so disturbed me.

I had allowed other people to think he was dead.

I had allowed him to be buried alive.

Another such flag: there had come a point (late February, early March, after Quintana had left the hospital but before the funeral that had waited on her recovery) when it had occurred to me that I was supposed to give John's clothes away. Many people had mentioned the necessity for giving the clothes away, usually in the well-intentioned but (as it turns out) misguided form of offering to help me do this. I had resisted. I had no idea why. I myself remembered, after my father died, helping my mother separate his clothes into stacks for Goodwill and "better" stacks for the charity thrift shop where my sister-in-law Gloria volunteered. After my mother died Gloria and I and Quintana and Gloria and Jim's daughters had done the same with her clothes. It was part of what people did after a death, part of the ritual, some kind of duty.

I began. I cleared a shelf on which John had stacked sweatshirts, T-shirts, the clothes he wore when we walked in Central Park in the early morning. We walked every morning. We did not always walk together because we liked different routes but we would keep the other's route in mind and intersect before we left the park. The clothes on this shelf were as familiar to me as my own. I closed my mind to this. I set aside certain things (a faded sweatshirt I particularly remembered him wearing, a Canyon Ranch T-shirt Quintana had brought him from Arizona), but I put most of what was on this shelf into bags and took the bags across the street to St. James' Episcopal Church. Emboldened, I opened a closet and filled more bags: New Balance sneakers, all-weather shoes, Brooks Brothers shorts, bag after bag of socks. I took the bags to St. James'. One day a few weeks later I gathered up more bags and took them to John's office, where he had kept his clothes. I was not yet prepared to address the suits and shirts and jackets but I thought I could handle what remained of the shoes, a start.

I stopped at the door to the room.

I could not give away the rest of his shoes.

I stood there for a moment, then realized why: he would need shoes if he was to return.

The recognition of this thought by no means eradicated the thought.

I have still not tried to determine (say, by giving away the shoes) if the thought has lost its power.

On reflection I see the autopsy itself as the first example of this kind of thinking. Whatever else had been in my mind when I so determinedly authorized an autopsy, there was also a level of derangement on which I reasoned that an autopsy could show that what had gone wrong was something simple. It could have been no more than a transitory blockage or arrhythmia. It could have required only a minor adjustment—a change in medication, say, or the resetting of a pacemaker. In this case, the reasoning went, they might still be able to fix it.

I recall being struck by an interview, during the 2004 campaign, in which Teresa Heinz Kerry talked about the sudden death of her first husband. After the plane crash

that killed John Heinz, she said in the interview, she had
felt very strongly that she "needed" to leave Washington
and go back to Pittsburgh.

Of course she "needed" to go back to Pittsburgh.

Pittsburgh, not Washington, was the place to which he
might come back.

The autopsy did not in fact take place the night John
was declared dead.

The autopsy did not take place until eleven the next
morning. I realize now that the autopsy could have taken
place only after the man I did not know at New York
Hospital made the phone call to me, on the morning of
December 31. The man who made the call was not "my
social worker," not "my husband's doctor," not, as John
and I might have said to each other, our friend from the
bridge. "Not our friend from the bridge" was family
shorthand, having to do with how his Aunt Harriet Burns
described subsequent sightings of recently encountered
strangers, for example seeing outside the Friendly's in
West Hartford the same Cadillac Seville that had earlier
cut her off on the Bulkeley Bridge. "Our friend from the
bridge," she would say. I was thinking about John saying
"not our friend from the bridge" as I listened to the man
on the telephone. I recall expressions of sympathy. I recall offers of assistance. He seemed to be avoiding some
point.

He was calling, he said then, to ask if I would donate
my husband's organs.

Many things went through my mind at this instant. The first word that went through my mind was "no." Simultaneously I remembered Quintana mentioning at dinner one night that she had identified herself as an organ donor when she renewed her driver's license. She had asked John if he had. He had said no. They had discussed it.

I had changed the subject.

I had been unable to think of either of them dead.

The man on the telephone was still talking. I was thinking: If she were to die today in the ICU at Beth Israel North, would this come up? What would I do? What would I do now?

I heard myself saying to the man on the telephone that my husband's and my daughter was unconscious. I heard myself saying that I did not feel capable of making such a decision before our daughter even knew he was dead. This seemed to me at the time a reasonable response.

Only after I hung up did it occur to me that nothing about it was reasonable. This thought was immediately (and usefully—notice the instant mobilization of cognitive white cells) supplanted by another: there had been in this call something that did not add up. There had been a contradiction in it. This man had been talking about donating organs, but there was no way at this point to do a productive organ harvest: John had not been on life support. He had not been on life support when I saw him in the curtained cubicle in the emergency room. He had not been on life support when the priest came. All organs would have shut down.

Then I remembered: the Miami-Dade Medical Examiner's office. John and I had been there together one morning in 1985 or 1986. There had been someone from the eye bank tagging bodies for cornea removal. Those bodies in the Miami-Dade Medical Examiner's office had not been on life support. This man from New York Hospital, then, was talking about taking only the corneas, the eyes. *Then why not say so? Why misrepresent this to me? Why make this call and not just say "his eyes"?* I took the silver clip the social worker had given me the night before from the box in the bedroom and looked at the driver's license. *Eyes: BL,* the license read. *Restrictions: Corrective Lenses.*

Why make this call and not just say what you wanted? His eyes. His blue eyes. His blue imperfect eyes.

> *and what i want to know is*
> *how do you like your blueeyed boy*
> *Mister Death*

I could not that morning remember who wrote those lines. I thought it was E. E. Cummings but I could not be sure. I did not have a volume of Cummings but found an anthology on a poetry shelf in the bedroom, an old textbook of John's, published in 1949, when he would have been at Portsmouth Priory, the Benedictine boarding school near Newport to which he was sent after his father died.

(His father's death: sudden, cardiac, in his early fifties, I should have taken that warning.)

If we happened to be anywhere around Newport John would take me to Portsmouth to hear the Gregorian chant at vespers. It was something that moved him. On the flyleaf of the anthology there was written the name *Dunne*, in small careful handwriting, and then, in the same handwriting, blue ink, fountain-pen blue ink, these guides to study: *1) What is the meaning of the poem and what is the experience? 2) What thought or reflection does the experience lead us to? 3) What <u>mood, feeling, emotion</u> is stirred or created by the poem as a whole?* I put the book back on the shelf. It would be some months before I remembered to confirm that the lines were in fact E. E. Cummings. It would also be some months before it occurred to me that my anger at this unknown caller from New York Hospital reflected another version of the primitive dread that had not for me been awakened by the autopsy question.

What was the meaning and what the experience?

To what thought or reflection did the experience lead us?

How could he come back if they took his organs, how could he come back if he had no shoes?

4.

On most surface levels I seemed rational. To the average observer I would have appeared to fully understand that death was irreversible. I had authorized the autopsy. I had arranged for cremation. I had arranged for his ashes to be picked up and taken to the Cathedral of St. John the Divine, where, once Quintana was awake and well enough to be present, they would be placed in the chapel off the main altar where my brother and I had placed our mother's ashes. I had arranged for the marble plate on which her name was cut to be removed and recut to include John's name. Finally, on the 23rd of March, almost three months after his death, I had seen the ashes placed in the wall and the marble plate replaced and a service held.

We had Gregorian chant, for John.

Quintana asked that the chant be in Latin. John too would have asked that.

We had a single soaring trumpet.

We had a Catholic priest and an Episcopal priest.

Calvin Trillin spoke, David Halberstam spoke, Quintana's best friend Susan Traylor spoke. Susanna Moore read a fragment from "East Coker," the part about how "one has only learnt to get the better of words / For the thing one no longer has to say, or the way in which / One is no longer disposed to say it." Nick read Catullus, "On His Brother's Death." Quintana, still weak but her voice steady, standing in a black dress in the same cathedral where she had eight months before been married, read a poem she had written to her father.

I had done it. I had acknowledged that he was dead. I had done this in as public a way as I could conceive.

Yet my thinking on this point remained suspiciously fluid. At dinner in the late spring or early summer I happened to meet a prominent academic theologian. Someone at the table raised a question about faith. The theologian spoke of ritual itself being a form of faith. My reaction was unexpressed but negative, vehement, excessive even to me. Later I realized that my immediate thought had been: *But I did the ritual. I did it all.* I did St. John the Divine, I did the chant in Latin, I did the Catholic priest and the Episcopal priest, I did "For a thousand years in thy sight are but as yesterday when it is past" and I did *"In paradisum deducant angeli."*

And it still didn't bring him back.

"Bringing him back" had been through those months my hidden focus, a magic trick. By late summer I was beginning to see this clearly. "Seeing it clearly" did not yet allow me to give away the clothes he would need.

In time of trouble, I had been trained since childhood, read, learn, work it up, go to the literature. Information was control. Given that grief remained the most general of afflictions its literature seemed remarkably spare. There was the journal C. S. Lewis kept after the death of his wife, *A Grief Observed*. There was the occasional passage in one or another novel, for example Thomas Mann's description in *The Magic Mountain* of the effect on Hermann Castorp of his wife's death: "His spirit was troubled; he shrank within himself; his benumbed brain made him blunder in his business, so that the firm of Castorp and Son suffered sensible financial losses; and the next spring, while inspecting warehouses on the windy landing-stage, he got inflammation of the lungs. The fever was too much for his shaken heart, and in five days, notwithstanding all Dr. Heidekind's care, he died." There were, in classical ballets, the moments when one or another abandoned lover tries to find and resurrect one or another loved one, the blued light, the white tutus, the *pas de deux* with the loved one that foreshadows the final return to the dead: *la danse des ombres,* the dance of the shades. There were certain poems, in fact many poems. There was a day or two when I relied on Matthew Arnold, "The Forsaken Merman":

> *Children's voices should be dear*
> *(Call once more) to a mother's ear;*
> *Children's voices, wild with pain—*
> *Surely she will come again!*

There were days when I relied on W. H. Auden, the "Funeral Blues" lines from *The Ascent of F6:*

> *Stop all the clocks, cut off the telephone,*
> *Prevent the dog from barking with a juicy bone,*
> *Silence the pianos and with muffled drum*
> *Bring out the coffin, let the mourners come.*

The poems and the dances of the shades seemed the most exact to me.

Beyond or below such abstracted representations of the pains and furies of grieving, there was a body of sub-literature, how-to guides for dealing with the condition, some "practical," some "inspirational," most of either useless. (Don't drink too much, don't spend the insurance money redecorating the living room, join a support group.) That left the professional literature, the studies done by the psychiatrists and psychologists and social workers who came after Freud and Melanie Klein, and quite soon it was to this literature that I found myself turning. I learned from it many things I already knew, which at a certain point seemed to promise comfort, validation, an outside opinion that I was not imagining what appeared to be happening. From *Bereavement: Reactions, Consequences, and Care,* compiled in 1984 by the National Academy of Sciences' Institute of Medicine, I learned for example that the most frequent immediate responses to death were shock, numbness, and a sense of disbelief: "Subjectively, survivors may feel like they are wrapped in a cocoon or blanket; to others, they may look as though they are holding up well. Because the reality of death has not yet penetrated awareness, survivors can appear to be quite accepting of the loss."

Here, then, we had the "pretty cool customer" effect.

I read on. Dolphins, I learned from J. William Worden of the Harvard Child Bereavement Study at Massachusetts General Hospital, had been observed refusing to eat after the death of a mate. Geese had been observed reacting to such a death by flying and calling, searching until they themselves became disoriented and lost. Human beings, I read but did not need to learn, showed similar patterns of response. They searched. They stopped eating. They forgot to breathe. They grew faint from lowered oxygen, they clogged their sinuses with unshed tears and ended up in otolaryngologists' offices with obscure ear infections. They lost concentration. "After a year I could read headlines," I was told by a friend whose husband had died three years before. They lost cognitive ability on all scales. Like Hermann Castorp they blundered in business and suffered sensible financial losses. They forgot their own telephone numbers and showed up at airports without picture ID. They fell sick, they failed, they even, again like Hermann Castorp, died.

This "dying" aspect had been documented, in study after study.

I began carrying identification when I walked in Central Park in the morning, in case it happened to me.

If the telephone rang when I was in the shower I no longer answered it, to avoid falling dead on the tile.

Certain studies, I learned, were famous. They were icons of the literature, benchmarks, referred to in everything I read. There was for example "Young, Benjamin, and Wallis, *The Lancet* 2:454–456, 1963." This study of 4,486 recent widowers in the United Kingdom, followed for five years, showed "significantly higher death rates for widowers in first six months following bereavement than for married." There was "Rees and Lutkins, *British Medical Journal* 4:13–16, 1967." This study of 903 bereaved relatives versus 878 non-bereaved matched controls, followed for six years, showed "significantly higher mortality for bereaved spouses in first year." The functional explanation for such raised mortality rates was laid out in the Institute of Medicine's 1984 compilation: "Research to date has shown that, like many other stressors, grief frequently leads to changes in the endocrine, immune, autonomic nervous, and cardiovascular systems; all of these are fundamentally influenced by brain function and neurotransmitters."

There were, I also learned from this literature, two kinds of grief. The preferred kind, the one associated with "growth" and "development," was "uncomplicated grief," or "normal bereavement." Such uncomplicated grief, according to *The Merck Manual,* 16th Edition, could still typically present with "anxiety symptoms such as initial insomnia, restlessness, and autonomic nervous system hyperactivity," but did "not generally cause clinical depression, except in those persons inclined to mood disorder." The second kind of grief was "complicated grief," which was also known in the literature as "pathological bereavement" and was said to occur in a variety of situations. One situation in which pathological bereavement could occur, I read repeatedly, was that in which the survivor and the deceased had been unusually dependent on one another. "Was the bereaved actually very dependent upon the deceased person for pleasure, support, or esteem?" This was one of the diagnostic criteria suggested by David Peretz, M.D., of the Department of Psychiatry at Columbia University. "Did the bereaved feel helpless without the lost person when enforced separations occurred?"

I considered these questions.

Once in 1968 when I needed unexpectedly to spend the night in San Francisco (I was doing a piece, it was raining, the rain pushed a late-afternoon interview into the next morning), John flew up from Los Angeles so that we could have dinner together. We had dinner at Ernie's. After dinner John took the PSA "Midnight Flyer," a thirteen-dollar amenity of an era in California when it was possible to fly from Los Angeles to San Francisco or Sacramento or San Jose for twenty-six dollars round-trip, back to LAX.

I thought about PSA.

All PSA planes had smiles painted on their noses. The flight attendants were dressed in the style of Rudy Gernreich in hot-pink-and-orange miniskirts. PSA represented a time in our life when most things we did seemed without consequence, no-hands, a mood in which no one thought twice about flying seven hundred miles for dinner. This mood ended in 1978, when a PSA Boeing 727 collided with a Cessna 172 over San Diego, killing one hundred and forty-four.

It occurred to me when this happened that I had overlooked the odds when it came to PSA.

I see now that this error was not confined to PSA.

When Quintana at age two or three flew PSA to Sacramento to see my mother and father she referred to it as "going on the smile." John used to write down the things she said on scraps of paper and put them in a black painted box his mother had given him. This box, which remains with its scraps of paper on a desk in my living room, was painted with an American eagle and the words "E Pluribus Unum." Later he used some of the things she said in a novel, *Dutch Shea, Jr.* He gave them to Dutch Shea's daughter, Cat, who had been killed by an IRA bomb while having dinner with her mother in a restaurant on Charlotte Street in London. This is part of what he wrote:

> "Where you was?" she would say, and "Where did the morning went?" He wrote them all down and crammed them into the tiny secret drawer in the maple desk Barry Stukin had given him and Lee as a wedding present. . . . Cat in her school tartan. Cat who could call her bath a "bathment" and the butterflies for a kindergarten experiment "flybutters." Cat who had made up her first poem at the age of seven: "I'm going to marry / A boy named Harry / He rides horses / And handles divorces."

> The Broken Man was in that drawer. The Broken Man was what Cat called fear and death and the unknown. I had a bad dream about the Broken

Man, she would say. Don't let the Broken Man
catch me. If the Broken Man comes, I'll hang onto
the fence and won't let him take me. . . . He wondered if the Broken Man had time to frighten Cat
before she died.

I see now what I had failed to see in 1982, the year
Dutch Shea, Jr. was published: this was a novel about
grief. The literature would have said that Dutch Shea
was undergoing pathological bereavement. The diagnostic signs would have been these: He is obsessed with the
moment Cat died. He plays and replays the scene, as if
rerunning it could reveal a different ending: the restaurant on Charlotte Street, the endive salad, Cat's lavender
espadrilles, the bomb, Cat's head in the dessert trolley.
He tortures his ex-wife, Cat's mother, with a single repeated question: why was she in the ladies' room when
the bomb went off? Finally she tells him:

> You never gave me much credit for being Cat's
> mother, but I did raise her. I took care of her the
> day she got her period the first time and I remem-
> ber when she was a little girl she called my bed-
> room her sweet second room and she called
> spaghetti buzzghetti and she called people who
> came to the house hellos. She said where you was
> and where did the morning went and you told
> Thayer, you son of a bitch, you wanted someone to

remember her. So she told me she was pregnant, it
was an accident, and she wanted to know what to
do and I went into the ladies' room because I knew
I was going to cry and I didn't want to cry in front of
her and I wanted to get the tears out of the way so I
could act sensibly and then I heard the bomb and
when I finally got out part of her was in the sherbet
and part of her was in the street and you, you son of
a bitch, you want someone to remember her.

I believe John would have said that *Dutch Shea, Jr.*
was about faith.

When he began the novel he already knew what the
last words would be, not only the last words of the novel
but the last words thought by Dutch Shea before he
shoots himself: "I believe in Cat. I believe in God." *Credo
in Deum.* The first words of the Catholic catechism.

Was it about faith or was it about grief?

Were faith and grief the same thing?

Were we unusually dependent on one another the
summer we swam and watched *Tenko* and went to dinner
at Morton's?

Or were we unusually lucky?

If I were alone could he come back to me on the smile?

Would he say get a table at Ernie's?

PSA and the smile no longer exist, sold to US Airways
and then painted off the planes.

Ernie's no longer exists, but was briefly re-created by Alfred Hitchcock, for *Vertigo*. James Stewart first sees Kim Novak at Ernie's. Later she falls from the bell tower (also re-created, an effect) at Mission San Juan Bautista.

We were married at San Juan Bautista.

On a January afternoon when the blossoms were showing in the orchards off 101.

When there were still orchards off 101.

No. The way you got sideswiped was by going back. The blossoms showing in the orchards off 101 was the incorrect track.

For several weeks after it happened I tried to keep myself on the correct track (the narrow track, the track on which there was no going back) by repeating to myself the last two lines of "Rose Aylmer," Walter Savage Landor's 1806 elegy to the memory of a daughter of Lord Aylmer's who had died at age twenty in Calcutta. I had not thought of "Rose Aylmer" since I was an undergraduate at Berkeley, but now I could remember not only the poem but much of what had been said about it in whichever class I had heard it analyzed. "Rose Aylmer" worked, whoever was teaching this class had said, because the overblown and therefore meaningless praise for the deceased in the first four lines ("Ah, what avails the sceptred race! / Ah, what the form divine! / What every virtue, every grace! / Rose Aylmer, all were thine") gets brought into sudden, even shocking relief by "the hard sweet wisdom" of the last two lines, which suggest that mourning has its place but also its limits: "A night of memories and sighs / I consecrate to thee."

" 'A *night* of memories and sighs,' " I remembered the lecturer repeating. "*A night.* One night. It might be all night but he doesn't even say *all night,* he says *a night,* not a matter of a lifetime, a matter of some hours."

Hard sweet wisdom. Clearly, since "Rose Aylmer" had remained embedded in my memory, I believed it as an undergraduate to offer a lesson for survival.

December 30, 2003.

We had seen Quintana in the sixth-floor ICU at Beth Israel North.

Where she would remain for another twenty-four days.

Unusual dependency (is that a way of saying "marriage"? "husband and wife"? "mother and child"? "nuclear family"?) is not the only situation in which complicated or pathological grief can occur. Another, I read in the literature, is one in which the grieving process is interrupted by "circumstantial factors," say by "a delay in the funeral," or by "an illness or second death in the family." I read an explanation, by Vamik D. Volkan, M.D., a professor of psychiatry at the University of Virginia in Charlottesville, of what he called "re-grief therapy," a technique developed at the University of Virginia for the treatment of "established pathological mourners." In such therapy, according to Dr. Volkan, a point occurs at which:

we help the patient to review the circumstances of the death—how it occurred, the patient's reaction to the news and to viewing the body, the events of the funeral, etc. Anger usually appears at this point if the therapy is going well; it is at first diffused, then directed toward others, and finally directed toward the dead. Abreactions—what Bibring [E. Bibring, 1954, "Psychoanalysis and the Dynamic Psychotherapies," *Journal of the American Psychoanalytic Association* 2:745 ff.] calls "emotional reliving"—may then take place and demonstrate to the patient the actuality of his repressed impulses. Using our understanding of the psychodynamics involved in the patient's need to keep the lost one alive, we can then explain and interpret the relationship that had existed between the patient and the one who died.

But from where exactly did Dr. Volkan and his team in Charlottesville derive their unique understanding of "the psychodynamics involved in the patient's need to keep the lost one alive," their special ability to "explain and interpret the relationship that had existed between the patient and the one who died"? Were you watching *Tenko* with me and "the lost one" in Brentwood Park, did you go to dinner with us at Morton's? Were you with me and "the one who died" at Punchbowl in Honolulu four months before it happened? Did you gather up plumeria blossoms with us and drop them on the graves of the unknown dead from Pearl Harbor? Did you catch cold with us in the rain at the Jardin du Ranelagh in Paris a month before it happened? Did you skip the Monets with us and go to lunch at Conti? Were you with us when we left Conti and bought the thermometer, were you sitting on our bed at the Bristol when neither of us could figure how to convert the thermometer's centigrade reading into Fahrenheit?

Were you there?

No.

You might have been useful with the thermometer but you were not there.

I don't need to "review the circumstances of the death." I was there.

I didn't get "the news," I didn't "view" the body. I was there.

I catch myself, I stop.

I realize that I am directing irrational anger toward the entirely unknown Dr. Volkan in Charlottesville.

> Persons under the shock of genuine affliction are not only upset mentally but are all unbalanced physically. No matter how calm and controlled they seemingly may be, no one can under such circumstances be normal. Their disturbed circulation makes them cold, their distress makes them unstrung, sleepless. Persons they normally like, they often turn from. No one should ever be forced upon those in grief, and all over-emotional people, no matter how near or dear, should be barred absolutely. Although the knowledge that their friends love them and sorrow for them is a great solace, the nearest afflicted must be protected from any one or anything which is likely to overstrain nerves already at the threatening point, and none have the right to feel hurt if they are told they can neither be of use or be received. At such a time, to some people companionship is a comfort, others shrink from their dearest friends.

That passage is from Emily Post's 1922 book of etiquette, Chapter XXIV, "Funerals," which takes the reader from the moment of death ("As soon as death occurs, someone, the trained nurse usually, draws the blinds in the sick-room and tells a servant to draw all the blinds of the house") through seating instructions for those who attend the funeral: "Enter the church as quietly as possible, and as there are no ushers at a funeral, seat yourself where you approximately belong. Only a very intimate friend should take a position far up on the center aisle. If you are merely an acquaintance you should sit inconspicuously in the rear somewhere, unless the funeral is very small and the church big, in which case you may sit on the end seat of the center aisle toward the back."

This tone, one of unfailing specificity, never flags. The emphasis remains on the practical. The bereaved must be urged to "sit in a sunny room," preferably one with an open fire. Food, but "very little food," may be offered on a tray: tea, coffee, bouillon, a little thin toast, a poached egg. Milk, but only heated milk: "Cold milk is bad for someone who is already over-chilled." As for further nourishment, "The cook may suggest something that appeals usually to their taste—but very little should be offered at a time, for although the stomach may be empty, the palate rejects the thought of food, and digestion is never in best order." The mourner is prompted to practice economy as he or she accommodates the wearing of mourning: most existing garments, including leather shoes and straw hats, will "dye perfectly." Undertaking expenses should be checked in advance. A friend should be left in charge of the house during the funeral. The friend should see that the house is aired and displaced furniture put back where it belongs and a fire lit for the homecoming of the family. "It is also well to prepare a little hot tea or broth," Mrs. Post advised, "and it should be brought them upon their return without their being asked if they would care for it. Those who are in great distress want no food, but if it is handed to them, they will mechanically take it, and something warm to start digestion and stimulate impaired circulation is what they most need."

There was something arresting about the matter-of-fact wisdom here, the instinctive understanding of the physiological disruptions ("changes in the endocrine, immune, autonomic nervous, and cardiovascular systems") later catalogued by the Institute of Medicine. I am unsure what prompted me to look up Emily Post's 1922 book of etiquette (I would guess some memory of my mother, who had given me a copy to read when we were snowbound in a four-room rented house in Colorado Springs during World War Two), but when I found it on the Internet it spoke to me directly. As I read it I remembered how cold I had been at New York Hospital on the night John died. I had thought I was cold because it was December 30 and I had come to the hospital bare-legged, in slippers, wearing only the linen skirt and sweater into which I had changed to get dinner. This was part of it, but I was also cold because nothing in my body was working as it should.

Mrs. Post would have understood that. She wrote in a world in which mourning was still recognized, allowed, not hidden from view. Philippe Ariès, in a series of lectures he delivered at Johns Hopkins in 1973 and later published as *Western Attitudes toward Death: From the Middle Ages to the Present*, noted that beginning about 1930 there had been in most Western countries and particularly in the United States a revolution in accepted attitudes toward death. "Death," he wrote, "so omnipresent in the past that it was familiar, would be effaced, would disappear. It would become shameful and forbidden." The English social anthropologist Geoffrey Gorer, in his 1965 *Death, Grief, and Mourning*, had described this rejection of public mourning as a result of the increasing pressure of a new "ethical duty to enjoy oneself," a novel "imperative to do nothing which might diminish the enjoyment of others." In both England and the United States, he observed, the contemporary trend was "to treat mourning as morbid self-indulgence, and to give social admiration to the bereaved who hide their grief so fully that no one would guess anything had happened."

One way in which grief gets hidden is that death now occurs largely offstage. In the earlier tradition from which Mrs. Post wrote, the act of dying had not yet been professionalized. It did not typically involve hospitals. Women died in childbirth. Children died of fevers. Cancer was untreatable. At the time she undertook her book of etiquette, there would have been few American households untouched by the influenza pandemic of 1918. Death was up close, at home. The average adult was expected to deal competently, and also sensitively, with its aftermath. When someone dies, I was taught growing up in California, you bake a ham. You drop it by the house. You go to the funeral. If the family is Catholic you also go to the rosary but you do not wail or keen or in any other way demand the attention of the family. In the end Emily Post's 1922 etiquette book turned out to be as acute in its apprehension of this other way of death, and as prescriptive in its treatment of grief, as anything else I read. I will not forget the instinctive wisdom of the friend who, every day for those first few weeks, brought me a quart container of scallion-and-ginger congee from Chinatown. Congee I could eat. Congee was all I could eat.

5.

There was something else I was taught growing up in California. When someone appears to have died you find out for sure by holding a hand mirror to the mouth and nose. If there is no exhaled moisture the person is dead. My mother taught me that. I forgot it the night John died. *Is he breathing,* the dispatcher had asked me. *Just come,* I had said.

December 30, 2003.

We had seen Quintana in the sixth-floor ICU at Beth Israel North.

We had noted the numbers on the respirator.

We had held her swollen hand.

We still don't know which way this is going, one of the *ICU doctors had said.*

We had come home. The ICU did not reopen after evening rounds until seven so it must have been past eight.

We had discussed whether to go out for dinner or eat in.

I said I would build a fire, we could eat in.

I have no memory of what we meant to eat. I do remember throwing out whatever was on the plates and in the kitchen when I came home from New York Hospital.

You sit down to dinner and life as you know it ends.

In a heartbeat.

Or the absence of one.

During the past months I have spent a great deal of time trying first to keep track of, and, when that failed, to reconstruct, the exact sequence of events that preceded and followed what happened that night. "At a point between Thursday, December 18, 2003, and Monday, December 22, 2003," one such reconstruction began, "Q complained of 'feeling terrible,' flu symptoms, thought she had strep throat." This reconstruction, which was preceded by the names and telephone numbers of doctors to whom I spoke not only at Beth Israel but at other hospitals in New York and other cities, continued. The heart of it was this: On Monday, December 22, she went with a fever of 103 to the emergency room at Beth Israel North, which had at the time a reputation for being the least-crowded emergency room on the Upper East Side of Manhattan, and was diagnosed with the flu. She was told to stay in bed and drink liquids. No chest X-ray was taken. On December 23 and 24 her fever fluctuated between 102 and 103. She was too ill to come to dinner on Christmas Eve. She and Gerry canceled plans to spend Christmas night and a few days after with his family in Massachusetts.

On Christmas Day, a Thursday, she called in the morning and said she was having trouble breathing. Her breathing sounded shallow, labored. Gerry took her back to the emergency room at Beth Israel North, where X-rays showed a dense infiltrate of pus and bacteria in the lower lobe of her right lung. Her pulse was elevated, 150-plus. She was extremely dehydrated. Her white count was almost zero. She was given Ativan, then Demerol. Her pneumonia, Gerry was told in the emergency room, was "a 5 on a scale of 10, what we used to call 'walking pneumonia.'" There was "nothing serious" (this may have been what I wanted to hear), but it was nonetheless decided to admit her to a sixth-floor ICU for monitoring.

By the time she reached the ICU that evening she was agitated. She was further sedated, then intubated. Her temperature was now 104-plus. One hundred percent of her oxygen was being supplied by the breathing tube; she was not at that point capable of breathing on her own. Late the next morning, Friday, December 26, it was learned that there was now pneumonia on both lungs, and that this pneumonia was, despite the massive IV administration of azithromycin, gentamicin, clindamycin, and vancomycin, growing. It was also learned—or assumed, since her blood pressure was dropping—that she was entering or had entered septic shock. Gerry was asked to allow two further invasive procedures, first the insertion of an arterial line and then the insertion of a second line that would go close to the heart to deal with the blood pressure problem. She was given neosynephrine to support her blood pressure at 90-plus over 60-plus.

On Saturday, December 27, we were told that she was being given what was then still a new Eli Lilly drug, Xigris, which would continue for ninety-six hours, four days. "This costs twenty thousand dollars," the nurse said as she changed the IV bag. I watched the fluid drip into one of the many tubes that were then keeping Quintana alive. I looked up Xigris on the Internet. One site said that the survival rate for sepsis patients treated with Xigris was 69 percent, as opposed to 56 percent for patients not treated with Xigris. Another site, a business newsletter, said that Eli Lilly's "sleeping giant," Xigris, was "struggling to overcome its problems in the sepsis market." This seemed in some ways a positive prism through which to view the situation: Quintana was not the child who had been a deliriously happy bride five months before and whose chance of surviving the next day or two could now be calibrated at a point between 56 and 69 percent, she was "the sepsis market," suggesting that there was still a consumer choice to be made. By Sunday, December 28, it had been possible to imagine that the sepsis market's "sleeping giant" was kicking in: the pneumonia had not decreased in size, but the neo-synephrine supporting her blood pressure was stopped and the blood pressure was holding, at 95 over 40. On Monday, December 29, I was told by a physician's assistant that after his weekend absence he had come in that morning to find Quintana's condition "encouraging." I asked what exactly had encouraged him about her condition when he came in that morning. "She was still alive," the physician's assistant said.

On Tuesday, December 30, at 1:02 p.m. (according to the computer), I made these notes in anticipation of a conversation with one more specialist to whom I had placed a call:

Any effect on brain—from oxygen deficit? From high fever? From possible meningitis?

Several doctors have mentioned "not knowing if there is some underlying structure or blockage." Are they talking about a possible malignancy?

The assumption here is that this infection is bacterial—yet no bacteria has shown up in the cultures—is there any way of knowing it's not viral?

How does "flu" morph into whole-body infection?

The last question—*How does "flu" morph into whole-body infection?*—was added by John. By December 30 he had seemed fixed on this point. He had asked it many times in the preceding three or four days, of doctors and of physicians' assistants and of nurses and finally, most desperately, of me, and had never received an answer he found satisfactory. Something in this seemed to defy his understanding. Something in this defied my own understanding, but I was pretending that I could manage it. Here it was:

She had been admitted to the ICU on Christmas night.

She was in a hospital, we had kept telling each other on Christmas night. She was being taken care of. She would be safe where she was.

Everything else had seemed normal.

We had a fire. She would be safe.

Five days later everything outside the sixth-floor ICU at Beth Israel North still seemed normal: this was the part neither of us (although only John admitted it) could get past, one more case of maintaining a fixed focus on the clear blue sky from which the plane fell. There were still in the living room of the apartment the presents John and I had opened on Christmas night. There were still under and on a table in Quintana's old room the presents she had been unable to open on Christmas night because she was in the ICU. There were still on a table in the dining room the stacked plates and silver we had used on

Christmas Eve. There were still on an American Express bill that came that day charges from the November trip we had made to Paris. When we left for Paris Quintana and Gerry had been planning their first Thanksgiving dinner. They had invited his mother and sister and brother-in-law. They were using their wedding china. Quintana had come by to get my mother's ruby crystal glasses. We had called them on Thanksgiving Day from Paris. They were roasting a turkey and pureeing turnips.

"And then—gone."

How does "flu" morph into whole-body infection?

I see the question now as the equivalent of a cry of helpless rage, another way of saying *How could this have happened when everything was normal.* In the cubicle where Quintana lay in the ICU, her fingers and face swollen with fluid, her lips cracked by fever around the breathing tube, her hair matted and soaked with sweat, the numbers on the respirator that night indicated that she was now receiving only 45 percent of her oxygen through the tube. John had kissed her swollen face. "More than one more day," he had whispered, another part of our family shorthand. The reference was to a line from a movie, Richard Lester's *Robin and Marian.* "I love you more than even one more day," Audrey Hepburn as Maid Marian says to Sean Connery as Robin Hood after she has given them both the fatal potion. John had whispered this every time he left the ICU. On our way out we managed to maneuver a doctor into talking to us. We asked if the decrease in delivered oxygen meant that she was getting better.

There was a pause.

This was when the ICU doctor said it: "We're still not sure which way this is going."

The way this is going is up, I remember thinking.

The ICU doctor was still talking. "She's really very sick," he was saying.

I recognized this as a coded way of saying that she was expected to die but I persisted: *The way this is going is up. It's going up because it has to go up.*

I believe in Cat.

I believe in God.

"I love you more than one more day," Quintana said three months later standing in the black dress at St. John the Divine. "As you used to say to me."

We were married on the afternoon of January 30, 1964, a Thursday, at the Catholic Mission of San Juan Bautista in San Benito County, California. John wore a navy blue suit from Chipp. I wore a short white silk dress I had bought at Ransohoff's in San Francisco on the day John Kennedy was killed. Twelve-thirty p.m. in Dallas was still morning in California. My mother and I learned what happened only when we were leaving Ransohoff's for lunch and ran into someone from Sacramento. Since there were only thirty or forty people at San Juan Bautista on the afternoon of the wedding (John's mother, his younger brother Stephen, his brother Nick and Nick's wife Lenny and their four-year-old daughter, my mother and father and brother and sister-in-law and grandfather and aunt and a few cousins and family friends from Sacramento, John's roommate from Princeton, maybe one or two others), my intention for the ceremony had been to have no entrance, no "procession," to just stand up there and do it. "Principals emerge," I remember Nick saying helpfully: Nick got the plan, but the organist who had materialized did not, and suddenly I found myself on my father's arm, walking up the aisle and weeping behind my dark glasses. When the ceremony was over we drove to the lodge at Pebble Beach. There were little things to eat, champagne, a terrace that opened onto the Pacific, very simple. By way of a honeymoon we spent a few nights in a bungalow at the San Ysidro Ranch in Montecito and then, bored, fled to the Beverly Hills Hotel.

I had thought about that wedding on the day of Quintana's wedding.

Her wedding was simple too. She wore a long white dress and a veil and expensive shoes but her hair was in a thick braid down her back, as it had been when she was a child.

We sat in the choir at St. John the Divine. Her father walked her to the altar. There at the altar was Susan, her best friend in California since age three. There at the altar was her best friend in New York. There at the altar was her cousin Hannah. There was her cousin Kelley from California, reading a part of the service. There were the children of Gerry's stepdaughter, reading another part. There were the youngest children, small girls with leis, barefoot. There were watercress sandwiches, champagne, lemonade, peach-colored napkins to match the sorbet that came with the cake, peacocks on the lawn. She kicked off the expensive shoes and unpinned the veil. "Wasn't that just about perfect," she said when she called that evening. Her father and I allowed that it was. She and Gerry flew to St. Barth's. John and I flew to Honolulu.

July 26, 2003.

Four months and 29 days before she was admitted to the ICU at Beth Israel North.

Five months and four days before her father died.

During the first week or two after he died, at night, when the protective exhaustion would hit me and I would leave the relatives and friends talking in the living room and dining room and kitchen of the apartment and walk down the corridor to the bedroom and shut the door, I would avoid looking at the reminders of our early marriage that hung on the corridor walls. In fact I did not need to look, nor could I avoid them by not looking: I knew them by heart. There was a photograph of John and me taken on a location for *The Panic in Needle Park*. It was our first picture. We went with it to the Cannes festival. It was the first time I had ever been to Europe and we were traveling first-class on Twentieth Century–Fox and I boarded the plane barefoot, it was that period, 1971. There was a photograph of John and me and Quintana at Bethesda Fountain in Central Park in 1970, John and Quintana, age four, eating ice cream bars. We were in New York all that fall working on a picture with Otto Preminger. "She's in the office of Mr. Preminger who has no hair," Quintana advised a pediatrician who had asked where her mother was. There was a photograph of John and me and Quintana on the deck of the house we had in Malibu in the 1970s. The photograph appeared in *People*. When I saw it I realized that Quintana had taken advantage of a break in the day's shooting to apply, for the first time, eyeliner. There was a photograph Barry Farrell had taken of his wife, Marcia, sitting in a rattan chair in the house in Malibu and holding their then-baby daughter, Joan Didion Farrell.

Barry Farrell was now dead.

There was a photograph of Katharine Ross, taken by Conrad Hall during the Malibu period when she taught Quintana to swim by throwing a Tahitian shell in a neighbor's pool and telling Quintana the shell would be hers if she brought it up. This was a time, the early 1970s, when

Katharine and Conrad and Jean and Brian Moore and John and I traded plants and dogs and favors and recipes and would have dinner at one or another of our houses a couple of times a week.

I remember that we all made soufflés. Conrad's sister Nancy in Papeete had shown Katharine how to make them work without effort and Katharine showed me and Jean. The trick was a less strict approach than generally advised. Katharine also brought back Tahitian vanilla beans for us, thick sheaves tied with raffia.

We did crème caramel with the vanilla for a while but nobody liked to caramelize the sugar.

We talked about renting Lee Grant's house above Zuma Beach and opening a restaurant, to be called "Lee Grant's House." Katharine and Jean and I would take turns cooking and John and Brian and Conrad would take turns running the front. This Malibu survivalist plan got abandoned because Katharine and Conrad separated and Brian was finishing a novel and John and I went to Honolulu to do a rewrite on a picture. We worked a lot in Honolulu. No one in New York could ever get the time difference straight so we could work all day without the phone ringing. There was a point in the 1970s when I wanted to buy a house there, and took John to look at many, but he seemed to interpret actually living in Honolulu as a less encouraging picture than staying at the Kahala.

Conrad Hall was now dead.

Brian Moore was now dead.

From an earlier house, a great wreck of a house on Franklin Avenue in Hollywood that we rented with its many bedrooms and its sun porches and its avocado trees and its overgrown clay tennis court for $450 a month, there was a framed verse that Earl McGrath had written on the occasion of our fifth anniversary:

> *This is the story of John Greg'ry Dunne*
> *Who, with his wife Mrs. Didion Do,*
> *Was legally married with family of one*
> *And lived on Franklin Avenue.*
> *Lived with their beautiful child Quintana*
> *Also known as Didion D*
> *Didion Dunne*
> *And Didion Do.*
> *And Quintana or Didion D.*
> *A beautiful family of one Dunne Dunne Dunne*
> *(I mean a family of three)*
> *Living in a style best called erstwhile*
> *On Franklin Avenue.*

People who have recently lost someone have a certain look, recognizable maybe only to those who have seen that look on their own faces. I have noticed it on my face and I notice it now on others. The look is one of extreme vulnerability, nakedness, openness. It is the look of someone who walks from the ophthalmologist's office into the bright daylight with dilated eyes, or of someone who wears glasses and is suddenly made to take them off. These people who have lost someone look naked because they think themselves invisible. I myself felt invisible for a period of time, incorporeal. I seemed to have crossed one of those legendary rivers that divide the living from the dead, entered a place in which I could be seen only by those who were themselves recently bereaved. I understood for the first time the power in the image of the rivers, the Styx, the Lethe, the cloaked ferryman with his pole. I understood for the first time the meaning in the practice of suttee. Widows did not throw themselves on the burning raft out of grief. The burning raft was instead an accurate representation of the place to which their grief (not their families, not the community, not custom, *their grief*) had taken them. On the night John died we were thirty-one days short of our fortieth anniversary. You will have by now divined that the "hard sweet wisdom" in the last two lines of "Rose Aylmer" was lost on me.

I wanted more than a night of memories and sighs.

I wanted to scream.

I wanted him back.

6.

Several years ago, walking east on Fifty-seventh Street between Sixth and Fifth Avenues on a bright fall day, I had what I believed at the time to be an apprehension of death. It was an effect of light: quick sunlight dappling, yellow leaves falling (but from what? were there even trees on West Fifty-seventh Street?), a shower of gold, spangled, very fast, a falling of the bright. Later I watched for this effect on similar bright days but never again experienced it. I wondered then if it had been a seizure, or stroke of some kind. A few years before that, in California, I had dreamed an image that, when I woke, I knew had been death: the image was that of an ice island, the jagged ridge seen from the air off one of the Channel Islands, except in this case all ice, translucent, a blued white, glittering in the sunlight. Unlike dreams in which the dreamer is anticipating death, inexorably sentenced to die but not yet there, there was in this dream no dread. Both the ice island and the fall of the bright on West Fifty-seventh Street seemed on the contrary transcendent, more beautiful than I could say, yet there was no doubt in my mind that what I had seen was death.

Why, if those were my images of death, did I remain so unable to accept the fact that he had died? Was it because I was failing to understand it as something that had happened to him? Was it because I was still understanding it as something that had happened to me?

Life changes fast.

Life changes in the instant.

You sit down to dinner and life as you know it ends.

The question of self-pity.

You see how early the question of self-pity entered the picture.

One morning during the spring after it happened I picked up *The New York Times* and skipped directly from the front page to the crossword puzzle, a way of starting the day that had become during those months a pattern, the way I had come to read, or more to the point not to read, the paper. I had never before had the patience to work crossword puzzles, but now imagined that the practice would encourage a return to constructive cognitive engagement. The clue that first got my attention that morning was 6 Down, "Sometimes you feel like . . ." I instantly saw the obvious answer, a good long one that would fill many spaces and prove my competency for the day: "a motherless child."

Motherless children have a real hard time—
Motherless children have such a real hard time—
No.

6 Down had only four letters.

I abandoned the puzzle (impatience died hard), and the next day looked up the answer. The correct answer for 6 Down was "anut." "Anut?" A nut? Sometimes you feel like *a nut*? How far had I absented myself from the world of normal response?

Notice: the answer most instantly accessed ("a motherless child") was a wail of self-pity.

This was not going to be an easy failure of understanding to correct.

Avid its rush, that reeling blaze!
Where is my father and Eleanor?
Not where are they now, dead seven years,
But what they were then?

                    No more? No more?

— DELMORE SCHWARTZ,
        "Calmly We Walk Through This April's Day"

He believed he was dying. He told me so, repeatedly. I dismissed this. He was depressed. He had finished a

novel, *Nothing Lost,* which was caught in the predictable
limbo of a prolonged period between delivery and publication, and he was undergoing an equally predictable
crisis of confidence about the book he was then beginning, a reflection on the meaning of patriotism that had
not yet found its momentum. He had been dealing as well
through most of the year with a series of enervating medical issues. His cardiac rhythm had been slipping with
increasing frequency into atrial fibrillation. A normal
sinus rhythm could be restored by cardioversion, an out-
patient procedure in which he was given general anesthesia for a few minutes while his heart was electrically
shocked, but a change in physical status as slight as
catching a cold or taking a long plane flight could again
disrupt the rhythm. His last such procedure, in April
2003, had required not one but two shocks. The steadily
increasing frequency with which cardioversion had become necessary indicated that it was no longer a useful
option. In June, after a series of consultations, he had undergone a more radical cardiac intervention, a radio-
frequency ablation of the atrial-ventricular node and the
subsequent implantation of the Medtronic Kappa 900 SR
pacemaker.

During the course of the summer, buoyed by the pleasure of Quintana's wedding and by the apparent success
of the pacemaker, his mood had seemed to lift. In the fall
it dropped again. I recall a fight over the question of

whether we should go to Paris in November. I did not want to go. I said we had too much to do and too little money. He said he had a sense that if he did not go to Paris in November he would never again go to Paris. I interpreted this as blackmail. That settles it then, I said, we're going. He left the table. We did not speak in any meaningful way for two days.

In the end we went to Paris in November.

I tell you that I shall not live two days, Gawain said.

A few weeks ago at the Council on Foreign Relations at Sixty-eighth and Park I noticed someone across from me reading the *International Herald Tribune.* One more example of slipping onto the incorrect track: I am no longer at the Council on Foreign Relations at Sixty-eighth and Park but sitting across from John at breakfast in the dining room of the Bristol in Paris in November 2003. We are each reading the *International Herald Tribune,* hotel copies, with little stapled cards showing the weather for the day. The cards for each of those November mornings in Paris showed an umbrella icon. We walked in the rain at the Jardin du Luxembourg. We escaped from the rain into St. Sulpice. There was a mass in progress. John took communion. We caught cold in the rain at the Jardin du Ranelagh. On the flight back to New York John's muffler and my jersey dress smelled of wet wool. On takeoff he held my hand until the plane began leveling.

He always did.

Where did that go?

In a magazine I see a Microsoft advertisement that shows the platform of the Porte des Lilas metro station in Paris.

I found yesterday in the pocket of an unworn jacket a used metro ticket from that November trip to Paris. "Only Episcopalians 'take' communion," he had corrected me one last time as we left St. Sulpice. He had been correcting me on this point for forty years. Episcopalians "took," Catholics "received." It was, he explained each time, a difference in attitude.

> *Not where are they now, dead seven years,*
> *But what they were then?*

That last cardioversion: April 2003. The one that had required two shocks. I remember a doctor explaining why it was done under anesthesia. "Because otherwise they jump off the table," he said. December 30, 2003: the sudden jump when the ambulance crew was using the defibrillating paddles on the living room floor. Was that ever a heartbeat or was it just electricity?

The night he died or the night before, in the taxi between Beth Israel North and our apartment, he said several things that for the first time made me unable to readily dismiss his mood as depression, a normal phase of any writer's life.

Everything he had done, he said, was worthless.

I still tried to dismiss it.

This might not be normal, I told myself, but neither was the condition in which we had just left Quintana.

He said that the novel was worthless.

This might not be normal, I told myself, but neither was it normal for a father to see a child beyond his help.

He said that his current piece in *The New York Review,* a review of Gavin Lambert's biography of Natalie Wood, was worthless.

This might not be normal, but what in the past several days had been?

He said he did not know what he was doing in New York. "Why did I waste time on a piece about Natalie Wood," he said.

It was not a question.

"You were right about Hawaii," he said then.

He may have meant that I had been right a day or so before when I said that when Quintana got better (this was our code for "if she lives") we could rent a house on the Kailua beach and she could recuperate there. Or he may have meant that I had been right in the 1970s when I wanted to buy a house in Honolulu. I preferred at the time to think the former but the past tense suggested the latter. He said these things in the taxi between Beth Israel North and our apartment either three hours before he died or twenty-seven hours before he died, I try to remember which and cannot.

7.

Why did I keep stressing what was and was not normal, when nothing about it was?

Let me try a chronology here.

Quintana was admitted to the ICU at Beth Israel North on December 25, 2003.

John died on December 30, 2003.

I told Quintana that he was dead late on the morning of January 15, 2004, in the ICU at Beth Israel North, after the doctors had managed to remove the breathing tube and reduce sedation to a point at which she could gradually wake up. Telling her that day had not been the plan. The doctors had said that she would wake only intermittently, at first partially, and for a matter of days be able to absorb only limited information. If she woke and saw me she would wonder where her father was. Gerry and Tony and I had discussed this problem at length. We had decided that only Gerry should be with her when she first began to wake. She could focus on him, on their life together. The question of her father might not come up. I could see her later, maybe days later. I could tell her then. She would be stronger.

As planned, Gerry was with her when she first woke. As not planned, a nurse told her that her mother was outside in the corridor.

Then when is she coming in, she wanted to know.

I went in.

"Where's Dad," she whispered when she saw me.

Because three weeks of intubation had inflamed her vocal cords, even her whisper was barely audible. I told her what had happened. I stressed the history of cardiac problems, the long run of luck that had finally caught up with us, the apparent suddenness but actual inevitability of the event. She cried. Gerry and I each held her. She dropped back into sleep.

"How's Dad," she whispered when I saw her that evening.

I began again. The heart attack. The history. The apparent suddenness of the event.

"But how is he *now*," she whispered, straining to be audible.

She had absorbed the sudden event part but not the outcome.

I told her again. In the end I would have to tell her a third time, in another ICU, this one at UCLA.

The chronology.

On January 19, 2004, she was moved from the sixth-floor ICU at Beth Israel North to a room on the twelfth floor. On January 22, 2004, still too weak to stand or sit unsupported and running a fever from a hospital infection acquired in the ICU, she was discharged from Beth Israel North. Gerry and I put her to bed in her old room in my apartment. Gerry went out to fill the prescriptions she had been given. She got out of bed to get another quilt from the closet and collapsed on the floor. I could not lift her and needed to get someone from the building to put her back to bed.

On the morning of January 25, 2004, she woke, still in my apartment, with severe chest pain and increasing fever. She was admitted that day to the Milstein Hospital at Columbia-Presbyterian after a diagnosis of pulmonary emboli was reached in the Presbyterian emergency room. Given her prolonged immobility at Beth Israel, I know now but did not know then, this was an entirely predictable development that could have been diagnosed before discharge from Beth Israel by the same imaging that was done three days later in the Presbyterian emergency room. After she was admitted to Milstein her legs were imaged to see if further clots had formed. She was placed on anticoagulants to prevent such further formation while the existing clots were allowed to dissolve.

On February 3, 2004, she was discharged from Presbyterian, still on anticoagulants. She began physical therapy to regain strength and mobility. Together, with Tony and Nick, she and I planned the service for John.

The service took place at four o'clock on a Tuesday afternoon, March 23, 2004, at the Cathedral of St. John
the Divine, where, at three o'clock in the presence of the
family, John's ashes had been placed as planned in the
chapel off the main altar. After the service Nick had
arranged a reception at the Union Club. Eventually thirty
or forty members of the family made their way back to
John's and my apartment. I lit a fire. We had drinks. We
had dinner. Quintana, although still fragile, had stood up
in her black dress at the Cathedral and laughed with her
cousins at dinner. On the morning of March 25, a day and
a half later, she and Gerry were going to restart their life
by flying to California and walking on the beach at
Malibu for a few days. I had encouraged this. I wanted to
see Malibu color on her face and hair again.

The next day, March 24, alone in the apartment, the
obligation to bury my husband and see our daughter
through her crisis formally fulfilled, I put away the plates
and allowed myself to think for the first time about what
would be required to restart my own life. I called
Quintana to wish her a good trip. She was flying early the
next morning. She sounded anxious. She was always anxious before a trip. Decisions about what to pack had
seemed since childhood to trigger some fear of lost orga-
nization. Do you think I'll be okay in California, she said.
I said yes. Definitely she would be okay in California.
Going to California would in fact be the first day of the
rest of her life. It occurred to me as I hung up that clean-

ing my office could be a step toward the first day of the rest of my own life. I began doing this. During most of the following day, Thursday, March 25, I continued doing this. At points during the quiet day I found myself thinking that possibly I had come through into a new season. In January I had watched ice floes form on the East River from a window at Beth Israel North. In February I had watched ice floes break up on the Hudson from a window at Columbia-Presbyterian. Now in March the ice was gone and I had done what I had to do for John and Quintana would come back from California restored. As the afternoon progressed (her plane would have landed, she would have picked up a car and driven up the Pacific Coast Highway) I imagined her already walking on the beach with Gerry in the thin March Malibu sunlight. I typed the Malibu zip code, 90265, into AccuWeather. There was sun, a high and low I do not remember but do remember thinking satisfactory, a good day in Malibu.

There would be wild mustard on the hills.

She could take him to see the orchids at Zuma Canyon.

She could take him to eat fried fish at the Ventura County line.

She had arranged to take him to lunch one day at Jean Moore's, she would be in the places in which she had spent her childhood. She could show him where we had gathered mussels for Easter lunch. She could show him where the butterflies were, where she had learned to play tennis, where she had learned from the Zuma Beach lifeguards how to swim out of a riptide. On the desk in my office there was a photograph taken when she was seven or eight, her hair long and blonde from the Malibu sun. Stuck in the back of the frame there was a crayoned note, left one day on the kitchen counter in Malibu: *Dear Mom, when you opened the door it was me who ran away XXXXXX —Q.*

At ten minutes past seven that evening I was changing to go downstairs, for dinner with friends who live in the building. I say "at ten minutes past seven" because that was when the phone rang. It was Tony. He said he was coming right over. I noted the time because I was due downstairs at seven-thirty but Tony's urgency was such that I did not say so. His wife, Rosemary Breslin, had spent the past fifteen years dealing with an undiagnosable blood disorder. Since shortly after John died she had been on an experimental protocol that had left her increasingly weak and required intermittent hospitalization at Memorial Sloan-Kettering. I knew that the long day at the Cathedral and later with the family had been strenuous for her. I stopped Tony as he was about to hang up. I asked if Rosemary was back in the hospital. He said it was not Rosemary. It was Quintana, who, even as we spoke, at ten minutes past seven in New York and ten minutes past four in California, was undergoing emergency neurosurgery at UCLA Medical Center in Los Angeles.

8.

They had gotten off the plane.

They had picked up their shared bag.

Gerry was carrying the bag to the car rental shuttle, crossing the arrivals driveway ahead of Quintana. He looked back. Even today I have no idea what made him look back. I never thought to ask. I pictured it as one more case in which you heard someone talking and then you didn't, so you looked. *Life changes in the instant. The ordinary instant.* She was lying on her back on the asphalt. An ambulance was called. She was taken to UCLA. According to Gerry she was awake and lucid in the ambulance. It was only in the emergency room that she began convulsing and lost coherence. A surgical team was alerted. A CT scan was done. By the time they took her into surgery one of her pupils was fixed. The other became fixed as they wheeled her in. I would be told this more than once, in each case as evidence of the gravity of the condition and the critical nature of the intervention: "One pupil was fixed and the other went as we wheeled her in."

The first time I heard this I did not know the significance of what I was being told. By the second time I did. Sherwin B. Nuland, in *How We Die,* described having seen, as a third-year medical student, a cardiac patient whose "pupils were fixed in the position of wide black dilatation that signifies brain death, and obviously would never respond to light again." Again in *How We Die,* Dr. Nuland described the failing attempts of a CPR team to revive a patient who had suffered cardiac arrest in the hospital: "The tenacious young men and women see their patient's pupils become unresponsive to light and then widen until they are large fixed circles of impenetrable blackness. Reluctantly the team stops its efforts. . . . The room is strewn with the debris of the lost campaign." Was this what the New York–Presbyterian ambulance crew saw in John's eyes on our living room floor on December 30, 2003? Was this what the UCLA neurosurgeons saw in Quintana's eyes on March 25, 2004? "Impenetrable blackness?" "Brain death?" Was that what they thought? I look at a printout of that day's CT report from UCLA and still go faint:

> The scan shows right hemispheric subdural hematoma, with evidence of acute bleeding. Active

bleeding cannot be excluded. The hematoma causes marked mass effect upon the right cerebrum, subfalcial and early uncal herniation, with 19 mm of midline shift from right to left at the level of the third ventricle. The right lateral ventricle is subtotally effaced and the left lateral ventricle shows early entrapment. There is moderate to marked midbrain compression and the perimesencephalic cistern is effaced. A thin posterior falcine and left tentorial subdural hematomas are noted. A small parenchymal bleed, likely contusional, is noted in the right inferolateral frontal lobe. The cerebellar tonsils are at the level of the foramen magnum. There is no skull fracture. There is a large right parietal scalp hematoma.

March 25, 2004. Ten minutes past seven in the evening in New York.

She had come back from the place where doctors said "We still don't know which way this is going" and now she was there again.

For all I knew it had already gone the wrong way.

They could have told Gerry and Gerry could be trying to absorb it before calling me.

She could already be on her way to the hospital morgue.

Alone. On a gurney. With a transporter.

I had already imagined this scene, with John.

Tony arrived.

He repeated what he had told me on the telephone. He had gotten the call from Gerry at UCLA. Quintana was in surgery. Gerry could be reached by cell phone in the hospital lobby, which happened to double (UCLA was building a new hospital, this one was overcrowded and outdated) as the surgical waiting area.

We called Gerry.

One of the surgeons had just come out to give him an update. The surgical team was now "fairly confident" that Quintana would "leave the table," although they could not predict in what condition.

I remember realizing that this was meant as an improved assessment: the previous report from the operating room had been that the team was "not at all sure she would leave the table."

I remember trying and failing to understand the phrase "leave the table." Did they mean alive? Had they said "alive" and Gerry could not say it? *Whatever happens,* I remember thinking, *she will without question "leave the table."*

It was then maybe four-thirty in Los Angeles, seven-thirty in New York. I was not sure how long at that point the surgery had been in progress. I see now, since according to the CT report the scan had taken place at "15:06," six minutes past three in Los Angeles, that she had probably been in surgery only about half an hour. I got out an OAG guide to see who would still be flying that night to Los Angeles. Delta had a 9:40 p.m. out of Kennedy. I was about to call Delta when Tony said that he did not think that being in flight during the surgery was a good idea.

I remember a silence.

I remember setting aside the OAG.

I called Tim Rutten in Los Angeles, and asked him to go to the hospital to wait with Gerry. I called our accountant in Los Angeles, Gil Frank, whose own daughter had undergone emergency neurosurgery at UCLA a few months before, and he too said that he would go to the hospital.

That was as close as I could get to being there.

I set the table in the kitchen and Tony and I picked at coq au vin left from the dinner for the family after St. John the Divine. Rosemary arrived. We sat at the kitchen table and tried to develop what we referred to as a "plan." We used phrases like "the contingencies," delicately, as if one of the three of us might not know what "the contingencies" were. I remember calling Earl McGrath to see if I could use his house in Los Angeles. I remember using the words "if I need to," another delicate construction. I remember him cutting directly through this: he was flying to Los Angeles the next day on a friend's plane, I would go with them. Around midnight Gerry called and said that the surgery was finished. They would now do another CT scan to see if there was additional bleeding they had missed. If there was bleeding they would oper-

ate again. If there was not they would do a further procedure, the placement of a screen in the vena cava to prevent clots from entering the heart. About four a.m. New
York time he called again, to say that the CT scan had
shown no bleeding and they had placed the screen. He
told me what the surgeons had told him about the operation itself. I made notes:

*"Arterial bleed, artery gushing blood, like a geyser,
blood all over the room, no clotting factor."*

"Brain pushed to the left side."

When I got back to New York from Los Angeles late on
the evening of April 30 I found these notes on a grocery
list by the kitchen phone. I now know that the technical
term for "brain pushed to the left side" is "midline shift,"
a significant predictive factor for poor outcome, but even
then I knew that it was not good. What I had thought I
needed on that March day five weeks before were Evian
splits, molasses, chicken broth, and flaxseed meal.

R*ead, learn, work it up, go to the literature.*
Information is control.

On the morning after the surgery, before I went to
Teterboro to get on the plane, I looked on the Internet for
"fixed and dilated pupils." I found that they were called

"FDPs." I read the abstract of a study done by researchers in the Department of Neurosurgery at the University Clinic in Bonn. The study followed ninety-nine patients who had either presented with or developed one or two FDPs. The overall mortality rate was 75 percent. Of the 25 percent who were still alive twenty-four months later, 15 percent had what the Glasgow Outcome Scale defined as an "unfavorable outcome" and 10 percent a "favorable outcome." I translated the percentages: of the ninety-nine patients, seventy-four died. Of the surviving twenty-five, at the end of two years, five were vegetative, ten were severely disabled, eight were independent, and two had made a full recovery. I also learned that fixed and dilated pupils indicated injury or compression of the third cranial nerve and the upper brainstem. "Third nerve" and "brainstem" were words that I would hear more often than I wanted to during the weeks to come.

9.

You're safe, I remember whispering to Quintana when I first saw her in the ICU at UCLA. *I'm here. You're going to be all right.* Half of her skull had been shaved for the surgery. I could see the long cut and the metal staples that held it closed. She was again breathing only through an endotracheal tube. *I'm here. Everything's fine.*

"When do you have to leave," she asked me on the day when she could finally speak. She said the words with difficulty, her face tensed.

I said I would not leave until we could leave together.

Her face relaxed. She went back to sleep.

It occurred to me during those weeks that this had been, since the day we brought her home from St. John's Hospital in Santa Monica, my basic promise to her. I would not leave. I would take care of her. She would be all right. It also occurred to me that this was a promise I could not keep. I could not always take care of her. I could not never leave her. She was no longer a child. She was an adult. Things happened in life that mothers could not prevent or fix. Unless one of those things killed her prematurely, as one had almost done at Beth Israel and another could still do at UCLA, I would die before she did. I remembered discussions in lawyers' offices during which I had become distressed by the word "predecease." The word could not possibly apply. After each of these discussions I would see the words "mutual disaster" in a new and favorable light. Yet once on a rough flight between Honolulu and Los Angeles I had imagined such a mutual disaster and rejected it. The plane would go down. Miraculously, she and I would survive the crash, adrift in the Pacific, clinging to the debris. The dilemma was this: I would need, because I was menstruating and the blood would attract sharks, to abandon her, swim away, leave her alone.

Could I do this?

Did all parents feel this?

When my mother was near death at age ninety she told me that she was ready to die but could not. "You and Jim need me," she said. My brother and I were by then in our sixties.

You're safe.

I'm here.

One thing I noticed during the course of those weeks at UCLA was that many people I knew, whether in New York or in California or in other places, shared a habit of mind usually credited to the very successful. They believed absolutely in their own management skills. They believed absolutely in the power of the telephone numbers they had at their fingertips, the right doctor, the major donor, the person who could facilitate a favor at State or Justice. The management skills of these people were in fact prodigious. The power of their telephone numbers was in fact unmatched. I had myself for most of my life shared the same core belief in my ability to control events. If my mother was suddenly hospitalized in Tunis I could arrange for the American consul to bring her English-language newspapers and get her onto an Air France flight to meet my brother in Paris. If Quintana was suddenly stranded in the Nice airport I could arrange with someone at British Airways to get her onto a BA flight to meet her cousin in London. Yet I had always at some level apprehended, because I was born fearful, that some events in life would remain beyond my ability to control or manage them. Some events would just happen. This was one of those events. *You sit down to dinner and life as you know it ends.*

Many people to whom I spoke in those first days while Quintana lay unconscious at UCLA seemed free of this apprehension. Their initial instinct was that this event could be managed. In order to manage it they needed only information. They needed only to know how this had happened. They needed answers. They needed "the prognosis."

I had no answers.

I had no prognosis.

I did not know how this had happened.

There were two possibilities, both of them, I came to see, irrelevant. One possibility was that she had fallen and the trauma had caused a bleed into her brain, a danger of the anticoagulants she had been given to prevent emboli. The second possibility was that the bleed into her brain had occurred before the fall and in fact caused it. People on anticoagulants bleed. They bruise at a touch. The level of anticoagulant in the blood, which is measured by a number called the INR (International Normalized Ratio), is hard to control. The blood must be tested every few weeks and in some cases every few days. Minute and complicated changes must be made in dosage. The ideal INR for Quintana was, give or take a tenth of a point, 2.2. On the day she flew to Los Angeles it so happened that her INR was over 4, a level at which spontaneous bleeding can occur. When I got to Los Angeles and spoke to the chief surgeon, he said that he was "one hundred percent sure" the trauma had caused the bleed. Other doctors to whom I spoke were less certain. It was suggested by one that the flight alone could have caused sufficient changes in pressurization to precipitate a bleed.

I recall pressing the surgeon on this point, myself trying (one more time) to manage the situation, get answers. I was talking to him on a cell phone from the courtyard outside the UCLA Medical Center cafeteria. The cafeteria was named "Café Med." This was my first visit to Café Med and my introduction to its most noticeable regular, a small balding man (I assumed a Neuropsychiatric Institute patient with walkaround privileges) whose compulsion it was to trail one or another woman through the cafeteria, alternately spitting and mouthing enraged imprecations about how disgusting she was, how vile, what a piece of worthless trash. On this particular morning the small balding man had trailed me out to the courtyard and it was hard to make out what the surgeon was saying. "It was the trauma, there was a ruptured blood vessel, we saw it," I thought he said. This had not seemed to entirely address the question—a ruptured blood vessel did not categorically rule out the possibility that the ruptured blood vessel had preceded and caused the fall—but there in the Café Med courtyard with the small balding man spitting on my shoe I realized that the answer to the question made no difference. It had happened. It was the new fact on the ground.

During the course of this call from the surgeon, which took place on the first full day I spent in Los Angeles, I recall being told several other things.

I recall being told that her coma could continue for days or weeks.

I recall being told that it would be a minimum of three days before anyone could begin to know what shape her brain was in. The surgeon was "optimistic," but no prediction was possible. Many more urgent issues could come up in the next three or four or more days.

She could develop an infection.

She could develop pneumonia, she could develop an embolism.

She could develop further swelling, which would necessitate reoperating.

After I hung up I walked back into the cafeteria, where Gerry was having coffee with Susan Traylor and my brother's daughters, Kelley and Lori. I remember wondering whether to mention the more urgent issues the surgeon had mentioned. I saw when I looked at their faces that there was no reason not to: all four of them had been at the hospital before I got to Los Angeles. All four of them had already heard about the more urgent issues.

During the twenty-four December and January nights when Quintana was in the sixth-floor ICU at Beth Israel North I had kept on the table by my bed a paperback copy of *Intensive Care: A Doctor's Journal,* by John F. Murray, M.D., who had been from 1966 to 1989 chief of the Pulmonary and Critical Care Division at the University of California medical school in San Francisco. *Intensive Care* describes, day by day, a four-week period in a San Francisco General Hospital medical ICU for which Dr. Murray was at the time the attending physician responsible for all patients, residents, interns, and medical students. I had read this account over and over. I had learned much that proved useful in the calibration of my daily dealings with the ICU doctors at Beth Israel North. I had learned for example that it was often difficult to gauge when the time was right for extubation, the removal of an endotracheal tube. I had learned that a common barrier to extubation was the edema so predictably seen in intensive care. I had learned that this edema was less often the result of an underlying pathology than of an excess in the administration of intravenous fluid, a failure to observe the distinction between hydration and overhydration, an error of caution. I had learned that many young residents made a similar error of caution

when it came to extubation itself: their tendency, because the outcome was uncertain, was to delay the procedure longer than necessary.

I had registered these lessons. I had made use of them:
the tentative question here, the expressed wish there. I
had "wondered" if she might not be "waterlogged." ("Of
course I don't know, I just know how she looks.") I had
deliberately used the word "waterlogged." I had noticed
a stiffening when I used the word "edema." I had further
"wondered" if she might not be better able to breathe if
she was less waterlogged. ("Of course I'm not a doctor,
but it just seems logical.") I had again "wondered" if the
monitored administration of a diuretic might not allow
extubation. ("Of course this is a home remedy, but if I felt
the way she looks I'd take a Lasix.") With *Intensive Care*
as my guide it had seemed straightforward, intuitive.
There was a way to know if you had made headway. You
knew you had made headway when a doctor to whom you
had made one or another suggestion presented, a day
later, the plan as his own.

This was different. A certain derisive phrase had occurred to me during the edema contest of wills at Beth
Israel North: *It's not brain surgery.* This was. When these
doctors at UCLA said "parietal" and "temporal" to me I
had no idea where in the brain they were talking about, let
alone what they meant. "Right frontal" I thought I could
understand. "Occipital" I thought suggested "eye," but
only on the misconceived reasoning that the word began

with "oc," like "ocular." I went to the UCLA Medical Center bookstore. I bought a book described on its cover as a "concise overview of neuroanatomy and of its functional and clinical implications" as well as an "excellent review for the USMLE." This book was by Stephen G. Waxman, M.D., chief of neurology at Yale–New Haven, and was called *Clinical Neuroanatomy.* I skimmed successfully through some of the appendices, for example "Appendix A: The Neurologic Examination," but when I began to read the text itself I could think only of a trip to Indonesia during which I had become disoriented by my inability to locate the grammar in Bahasa Indonesia, the official language used on street signs and storefronts and billboards. I had asked someone at the American Embassy how to tell the verbs from the nouns. Bahasa was a language, he had said, in which the same word could be either a verb or a noun. *Clinical Neuroanatomy* seemed to be one more case in which I would be unable to locate the grammar. I put it on the table by my bed at the Beverly Wilshire Hotel, where it would remain for the next five weeks.

On further study of *Clinical Neuroanatomy,* say if I woke in the morning before *The New York Times* had arrived with its sedative crossword puzzle, even "Appendix A: The Neurologic Examination" seemed opaque. I had originally noticed the obvious familiar directives (ask the patient the name of the president, ask the patient to count backwards from one hundred by sevens), but as days passed I seemed focused on a mysterious narrative, identified in Appendix A as the "gilded-boy story," that could be used to test memory and comprehension. The patient could be told the story, Dr. Waxman suggested, then asked to retell it in his own words and explain its meaning. "At the coronation of one of the popes, about 300 years ago, a little boy was chosen to play the part of an angel."

So began the "gilded-boy story."

So far clear enough, although potentially troubling details (three hundred years ago? play the part of an angel?) for someone emerging from coma.

It continued: "So that his appearance might be as magnificent as possible, he was covered from head to foot with a coating of gold foil. The little boy fell ill, and although everything possible was done for his recovery except the removal of the fatal golden covering, he died within a few hours."

What was the "meaning" of the "gilded-boy story"? Did it have to do with the fallibility of "the popes"? With the fallibility of authority in general? With the specific fallibility (note that "everything possible was done for his recovery") of medicine? What possible point could there be in telling this story to a patient immobilized in a neuro ICU at a major teaching hospital? What lesson could be drawn? Did they think that because it was a "story" it could be told without consequence? There was a morning on which the "gilded-boy story" seemed to represent, in its utter impenetrability and apparent disregard for the sensitivity of the patient, the entire situation with which I was faced. I went back to the UCLA Medical Center bookstore with the thought of checking other sources for an elucidation, but there was no mention of the gilded-boy story in the first several textbooks I picked up. In lieu of checking further, I bought, since the afternoon highs in Los Angeles were by then in the eighties and I had flown west with only the late-winter clothes I had been wearing in New York, several sets of blue cotton scrubs. So profound was the isolation in which I was then operating that it did not immediately occur to me that for the mother of a patient to show up at the hospital wearing blue cotton scrubs could only be viewed as a suspicious violation of boundaries.

10.

I had first noticed what I came to know as "the vortex effect" in January, when I was watching the ice floes form on the East River from a window at Beth Israel North. At the join between the walls and the ceiling of the room from which I was watching the ice floes there happened to be a rose-patterned wallpaper border, a Dorothy Draper touch, left I supposed from the period when what was then Beth Israel North had been Doctors' Hospital. I myself had never been in Doctors' Hospital, but when I was in my twenties and working for *Vogue* it had figured in many conversations. It had been the hospital favored by *Vogue* editors for uncomplicated deliveries and for "resting," a kind of medical Maine Chance.

This had seemed a good line of thinking.

This had seemed better than thinking about why I was at Beth Israel North.

I had ventured further:

Doctors' Hospital was where X had the abortion that was bought and paid for by the district attorney's office. "X" was a woman with whom I had worked at *Vogue.* Seductive clouds of cigarette smoke and Chanel No. 5 and imminent disaster had trailed her through the Condé Nast offices, which were then in the Graybar Building. On a single morning, while I was attempting to put together a particularly trying *Vogue* feature called "People Are Talking About," she had found both that she needed an abortion and that her name had turned up in the files of a party girl operation under investigation by the district attorney's office. She had been cheerful about these two pieces of (what had seemed to me) devastating news. A deal had been struck. She had agreed to testify that she had been approached by the operation, and the district attorney's office had in turn arranged a D&C at Doctors' Hospital, no inconsiderable favor at a time when getting an abortion meant making a clandestine and potentially lethal appointment with someone whose first instinct in a crisis would be to vacate the premises.

The party girl operation and the arranged abortion and the years in which I had spent mornings putting together "People Are Talking About" still seemed a good line of thinking.

I remembered having used such an incident in my second novel, *Play It As It Lays.* The protagonist, a for-

mer model named Maria, had recently had an abortion,
which was troubling her.

> Once a long time before Maria had worked a week
> in Ocho Rios with a girl who had just had an abor-
> tion. She could remember the girl telling her about
> it while they sat huddled next to a waterfall waiting
> for the photographer to decide the sun was high
> enough to shoot. It seemed that it was a hard time
> for abortions in New York, there had been arrests,
> no one wanted to do it. Finally the girl, her name
> was Ceci Delano, had asked a friend in the dis-
> trict attorney's office if he knew of anyone. "Quid
> pro quo," he had said, and, late the same day that
> Ceci Delano testified to a blue-ribbon jury that
> she had been approached by a party girl operation,
> she was admitted to Doctors' Hospital for a legal
> D&C, arranged and paid for by the district attor-
> ney's office.
>
> It had seemed a funny story as she told it, both
> that morning at the waterfall and later at dinner,
> when she repeated it to the photographer and the
> agency man and the fashion coordinator for the
> client. Maria tried now to put what had happened
> in Encino into the same spirited perspective, but
> Ceci Delano's situation seemed not to apply. In the
> end it was just a New York story.

This seemed to be working.

I had avoided thinking for at least two minutes about why I was at Beth Israel North.

I had moved on, into the period during which I was writing *Play It As It Lays.* The rented wreck of a house on Franklin Avenue in Hollywood. The votive candles on the sills of the big windows in the living room. The *té de limón* grass and aloe that grew by the kitchen door. The rats that ate the avocados. The sun porch on which I worked. Watching from the windows of the sun porch as Quintana ran through a sprinkler on the lawn.

I recall recognizing that I had hit more dangerous water but there had seemed no turning back.

I had been writing that book when Quintana was three. *When Quintana was three.*

There it was, the vortex.

Quintana at three. The night she had put a seed pod from the garden up her nose and I had driven her to Children's Hospital. The pediatrician who specialized in seed pods had arrived in his dinner jacket. The next night she had put another seed pod up her nose, wanting to repeat the interesting adventure. John and I walking with her around the lake in MacArthur Park. The old man lurching from a bench. "That child is the picture of Ginger Rogers," the old man cried. I finished the novel, I was under contract to begin a column for *Life,* we took Quintana to Honolulu. *Life's* idea for the first column was that I should introduce myself, "let the readers know who you are." I planned to write it from Honolulu, the Royal

Hawaiian Hotel, we used to get a lanai suite on the press rate for twenty-seven dollars a night. While we were there the news of My Lai broke. I thought about the first column. It seemed to me that given this news I should write it from Saigon. By then it was a Sunday. *Life* had given me a printed card with the home numbers of its editors and also of lawyers in cities around the world. I took out the card and called my editor, Loudon Wainwright, to say I was going to Saigon. His wife answered the phone. She said he would have to call me back.

"He's watching the NFL game," John said when I hung up. "He'll call you at halftime."

He did. He said that I should stay where I was and introduce myself, that as far as Saigon went "some of the guys are going out." The topic did not seem open to further discussion. "There's a world in revolution out there and we can put you in it," George Hunt had said when he was still the managing editor of *Life* and offering me the job. By the time I finished *Play It As It Lays* George Hunt had retired and some of the guys were going out.

"I warned you," John said. "I told you what working for *Life* would be like. Didn't I tell you? It would be like being nibbled to death by ducks?"

I was brushing Quintana's hair. The picture of Ginger Rogers.

I felt betrayed, humiliated. I should have listened to John.

I wrote the column letting the readers know who I was.

It appeared. At the time it seemed an unexceptional enough eight hundred words in the assigned genre, but there was, at the end of the second paragraph, a line so out of synch with the entire *Life* mode of self-presentation that it might as well have suggested abduction by space aliens: "We are here on this island in the middle of the Pacific in lieu of filing for divorce." A week later we happened to be in New York. "Did you know she was writing it," many people asked John, sotto voce.

Did he know I was writing it?

He edited it.

He took Quintana to the Honolulu Zoo so I could rewrite it.

He drove me to the Western Union office in downtown Honolulu so I could file it.

At the Western Union office he wrote *REGARDS, DIDION* at the end of it. That was what you always put at the end of a cable, he said. Why, I said. Because you do, he said.

See where that particular vortex sucked me.

From the Dorothy Draper wallpaper border at Beth Israel North to Quintana at three and I should have listened to John.

I tell you that I shall not live two days, Gawain said.

The way you got sideswiped was by going back.

I saw immediately in Los Angeles that its potential for triggering this vortex effect could be controlled only by avoiding any venue I might associate with either Quintana or John. This would require ingenuity. John and I had lived in Los Angeles County from 1964 until 1988. Between 1988 and the time he died we had spent significant amounts of time there, usually at the very hotel in which I was now staying, the Beverly Wilshire. Quintana was born in Los Angeles County, at St. John's Hospital in Santa Monica. She went to school there, first in Malibu and later at what was then still the Westlake School for Girls (the year after she left it became coeducational, and was called Harvard-Westlake) in Holmby Hills.

For reasons that remain unclear to me the Beverly Wilshire itself only rarely triggered the vortex effect. In theory its every corridor was permeated with the associations I was trying to avoid. When we were living in Malibu and had meetings in town we would bring Quintana and stay at the Beverly Wilshire. After we moved to New York and needed to be in Los Angeles for a picture we would stay there, sometimes for a few days, sometimes for weeks at a time. We set up computers and

printers there. We had meetings there. *What if,* someone
was always saying in these meetings. We could work
until eight or nine in the evening there and transmit the
pages to whichever director or producer we were working
with and then go to dinner at a Chinese restaurant on
Melrose where we did not need a reservation. We always
specified the old building. I knew the housekeepers. I
knew the manicurists. I knew the doorman who would
give John the bottled water when he came back from
walking in the morning. I knew by reflex how to work the
key and open the safe and adjust the shower head: I had
stayed over the years in some dozens of rooms identical to
the one in which I was now staying. I had last stayed in
such a room in October 2003, alone, doing promotion,
two months before John died. Yet the Beverly Wilshire
seemed when Quintana was at UCLA the only safe place
for me to be, the place where everything would be the
same, the place where no one would know about or refer
to the events of my recent life; the place where I would
still be the person I had been before any of this happened.

What if.

Outside the exempt zone that was the Beverly Wilshire, I plotted my routes, I remained on guard.

Never once in five weeks did I drive into the part of
Brentwood in which we had lived from 1978 until 1988.
When I saw a dermatologist in Santa Monica and street
work forced me to pass within three blocks of our house

in Brentwood, I did not look left or right. Never once in five weeks did I drive up the Pacific Coast Highway to Malibu. When Jean Moore offered me the use of her house on the Pacific Coast Highway, three-eighths of a mile past the house in which we had lived from 1971 until 1978, I invented reasons why it was essential for me to stay instead at the Beverly Wilshire. I could avoid driving to UCLA on Sunset. I could avoid passing the intersection at Sunset and Beverly Glen where for six years I had turned off to the Westlake School for Girls. I could avoid passing any intersection I could not anticipate, control. I could avoid keeping the car radio tuned to the stations I used to drive by, avoid locating KRLA, an AM station that had called itself "the heart and soul of rock and roll" and was still in the early 1990s programming the top hits of 1962. I could avoid punching in the Christian call-in station to which I had switched whenever the top hits of 1962 lost their resonance.

Instead I listened to NPR, a sedate morning show called *Morning Becomes Eclectic*. Every morning at the Beverly Wilshire I ordered the same breakfast, huevos rancheros with one scrambled egg. Every morning when I left the Beverly Wilshire I drove the same way to UCLA: out Wilshire, right on Glendon, slip left to Westwood, right on Le Conte and left at Tiverton. Every morning I noted the same banners fluttering from the light standards along Wilshire: *UCLA Medical Center—#1 in the West,*

#3 in the Nation. Every morning I wondered whose rank-
ing this was. I never asked. Each morning I inserted my
ticket into the gate mechanism and each morning, if I inserted it right, the same woman's voice said "*Wel*-come to
U-C-L-A." Each morning, if I timed it right, I got a parking place outside, on the Plaza 4 level, against the hedge.
Late each afternoon I would drive back to the Beverly
Wilshire, pick up my messages, and return a few of them.
After the first week Gerry was flying back and forth between Los Angeles and New York, trying to work at least
a few days a week, and if he was in New York I would call
to give him the day's information or lack of it. I would lie
down. I would watch the local news. I would stand in the
shower for twenty minutes and go out to dinner.

I went out to dinner every night I was in Los Angeles.
I had dinner with my brother and his wife whenever they
were in town. I went to Connie Wald's house in Beverly
Hills. There were roses and nasturtiums and open fires in
the big fireplaces, as there had been through all the years
when John and I and Quintana would go there. Now
Susan Traylor was there. I went to Susan's own house in
the Hollywood hills. I had known Susan since she was
three and I had known her husband Jesse since he and
Susan and Quintana were in the fourth grade at the Point
Dume School, and now they were looking after me. I ate
in many restaurants with many friends. I had dinner
quite often with Earl McGrath, whose intuitive kindness

in this situation was to ask me every morning what I was doing that night and, if the answer was in any way vague, to arrange an untaxing dinner for two or three or four at Orso or at Morton's or at his house on Robertson Boulevard.

After dinner I would take a taxi back to the hotel and place my morning order for huevos rancheros. "One scrambled egg," the voice on the phone would prompt. "Exactly," I would say.

I plotted these evenings as carefully as I plotted the routes.

I left no time to dwell on promises I had no way of keeping.

You're safe. I'm here.

In the deep hush of *Morning Becomes Eclectic* the next day I would congratulate myself.

I could have been in Cleveland.

Yet.

I cannot count the days on which I found myself driving abruptly blinded by tears.

The Santa Ana was back.

The jacaranda was back.

One afternoon I needed to see Gil Frank, at his office on Wilshire, several blocks east of the Beverly Wilshire. In this previously untested territory (*terra cognita* for these purposes was west on Wilshire, not east) I caught sight, unprepared, of a movie theater in which John and

I had in 1967 seen *The Graduate*. There had been no particular sense of moment about seeing *The Graduate* in 1967. I had been in Sacramento. John had picked me up at LAX. It had seemed too late to shop for dinner and too early to eat in a restaurant so we had gone to see *The Graduate* and then to dinner at Frascati's. Frascati's was gone but the theater was still there, if only to trap the unwary.

There were many such traps. One day I would notice a familiar stretch of coastal highway in a television commercial and realize it was outside the gate house, on the Palos Verdes Peninsula at Portuguese Bend, to which John and I had brought Quintana home from St. John's Hospital.

She was three days old.

We had placed her bassinet next to the wisteria in the box garden.

You're safe. I'm here.

Neither the house nor its gate could be seen in the commercial but I experienced a sudden rush of memories: getting out of the car on that highway to open the gate so that John could drive through; watching the tide come in and float a car that was sitting on our beach to be shot for a commercial; sterilizing bottles for Quintana's formula while the gamecock that lived on the property followed me companionably from window to window. This gamecock, named "Buck" by the owner of the house, had been abandoned on the highway, in the colorful opinion of the owner by "Mexicans on the run." Buck had a distinctive and surprisingly endearing personality, not unlike a Labrador. In addition to Buck this house also came equipped with peacocks, which were decorative but devoid of personality. Unlike Buck, the peacocks were fat and moved only as a last resort. At dusk they would scream and try to fly to their nests in the olive trees, a fraught moment because they would so often fall. Just before dawn they would scream again. One dawn I woke to the screaming and looked for John. I found him outside in the dark, tearing unripe peaches from a tree and hurling them at the peacocks, a characteristically straightforward if counterproductive approach to resolving an annoyance. When Quintana was a month old we were evicted. There was a clause in the lease that specified no children but the owner and his wife allowed that the baby was not the reason. The reason was that we had hired a pretty teenager named Jennifer to take care of her. The owner and his wife did not want strangers on the property, or as they said "behind the gate," particularly pretty teenagers named Jennifer, who would presumably have dates. We took a few months' lease on a house in town that belonged to Herman Mankiewicz's widow, Sara, who was going to be traveling. She left everything in the house as it was except one object, the Oscar awarded to Herman Mankiewicz for the screenplay of *Citizen Kane*.

"You'll have parties, people will just get drunk and play with it," she said when she put it away. On the day we moved John was traveling with the San Francisco Giants, doing a piece on Willie Mays for *The Saturday Evening Post.* I borrowed my sister-in-law's station wagon, loaded it, put Quintana and Jennifer in the back seat, said good-bye to Buck, drove out, and let the totemic gate lock behind me for the last time.

All that and I had not even driven down there.

All I had done was catch sight of a commercial on television while I was dressing to go to the hospital.

Another day I would need to buy bottled water at the Rite Aid on Canon and remember that Canon was where The Bistro had been. In 1964 and 1965, when we were living in the gate house with the beach and the peacocks but could not afford even to tip the parking boys at restaurants, let alone eat in them, John and I used to park on the street on Canon and charge dinner at The Bistro. We took Quintana there on the day of her adoption, when she was not quite seven months old. They had given us Sidney Korshak's corner banquette and placed her carrier on the table, a centerpiece. At the courthouse that morning she had been the only baby, even the only child; all the other adoptions that day had seemed to involve adults adopting one another for tax reasons. "*Qué bonita, qué hermosa,*" the busboys at The Bistro crooned when we brought her in at lunch. When she was six or seven we took her there for a birthday dinner. She was wearing a lime-green ruana I had bought for her in Bogotá. As we were about to leave the waiter had brought the ruana and she had flung it theatrically over her small shoulders.

Qué bonita, qué hermosa, the picture of Ginger Rogers.

John and I had been in Bogotá together. We had escaped from a film festival in Cartagena and gotten on an Avianca flight to Bogotá. An actor who had been at the film festival, George Montgomery, had also been on the flight to Bogotá. He had gone up to the cockpit. From where I was sitting I could see him chatting with the crew, then sliding into the pilot's seat.

I had nudged John, who was sleeping. "They're letting George Montgomery fly this plane over the Andes," I had whispered.

"It beats Cartagena," John said, and went back to sleep.

I did not that day on Canon get as far as the Rite Aid.

11.

Sometime in June, after she had left UCLA and was in the sixth of what would be fifteen weeks as an inpatient at the Rusk Institute of Rehabilitation Medicine at New York University Medical Center in New York, Quintana told me that her memory not only of UCLA but of her arrival at Rusk was "all mudgy." She could remember some things about UCLA, yes, as she could not yet remember anything else since before Christmas (she did not for example remember speaking about her father at St. John the Divine, nor, when she first woke at UCLA, did she remember that he had died), but it was still "mudgy." Later she corrected this to "smudgy," but she did not need to: I knew exactly what she meant. On the neuro floors at UCLA they had called it "spotty," as in "her orientation is improving but still spotty." When I try to reconstruct those weeks at UCLA I recognize the mudginess in my own memory. There are parts of days that seem very clear and parts of days that do not. I clearly remember arguing with a doctor the day they decided to do the tracheostomy. She had by then been intubated for almost a week, the doctor said. UCLA did not leave tubes in for more than a week. I said that she had been intubated for three weeks at Beth Israel in New York. The doctor had looked away. "The rule at Duke was also a week," he said, as if under the impression that mention of Duke would settle the question. Instead it enraged me: *What is Duke to me,* I wanted to say but did not. *What is Duke to UCLA. Duke is North Carolina. UCLA is California. If I wanted the opinion of somebody in North Carolina I would call somebody in North Carolina.*

Her husband is right now on a flight to New York, I said instead. Surely this can wait until he lands.

Not really, the doctor said. Since it's already on the schedule.

The day they decided to do the tracheostomy was also the day they turned off the EEG.

"Everything's looking good," they kept saying. "She's going to get better sooner once we do the trach. She's already off the EEG, maybe you didn't notice that."

Maybe I didn't notice that?

My only child?

My unconscious child?

Maybe I didn't notice when I walked into the ICU that

morning that her brain waves were gone? That the monitor above her bed was dark, dead?

This was now being presented as progress but it had not seemed so when I first saw it. I remembered reading in *Intensive Care* that the ICU nurses at San Francisco General turned off the monitors when a patient was near death, because their experience was that family members would focus on the screens rather than on the dying patient. I wondered if such a determination had been made in this case. Even after I was assured that this was not the case, I found myself averting my eyes from the blank EEG screen. I had grown used to watching her brain waves. It was a way of hearing her talk.

I did not see why, since the equipment was sitting there unused, they could not keep the EEG on.

Just in case.

I had asked.

I do not remember getting an answer. It was a period when I asked many questions that did not get answered. What answers I did get tended to the unsatisfactory, as in, "It's already on the schedule."

Everyone in the neuro units got a trach, they had kept saying to me that day. Everyone in the neuro units had muscular weaknesses that rendered the removal of the breathing tube problematic. A trach involved less risk of windpipe damage. A trach involved less risk of pneumonia. Look to your right, look to your left, both sides have trachs. A trach could be done with fentanyl and a muscle relaxant, she would be under anesthesia no more than an hour. A trach would leave no cosmetic effect to speak of, "only a little dimple scar," "as time goes by maybe no scar at all."

They kept mentioning this last point, as if the basis for my resistance to the trach was the scar. They were doctors, however freshly minted. I was not. Ergo, any concerns I had must be cosmetic, frivolous.

In fact I had no idea why I so resisted the trach.

I think now that my resistance came from the same fund of superstition from which I had been drawing since John died. If she did not have a trach she could be fine in the morning, ready to eat, talk, go home. If she did not have a trach we could be on a plane by the weekend. Even if they did not want her to fly, I could take her with me to the Beverly Wilshire, we could have our nails done, sit by the pool. If they still did not want her to fly we could drive out to Malibu, spend a few restorative days with Jean Moore.

If she did not have a trach.

This was demented, but so was I.

Through the printed blue cotton curtains that separated the beds I could hear people talking to their functionally absent husbands, fathers, uncles, co-workers. In the bed to Quintana's right was a man injured in a construction accident. The men who had been on the site at the time of the accident had come to see him. They stood around his bed and tried to explain what had happened. The rig, the cab, the crane, I heard a noise, I called out to Vinny. Each man gave his version. Each version differed slightly from the others. This was understandable, since each witness proceeded from a different point of view, but I recall wanting to intercede, help them coordinate their stories; it had seemed too much conflicting data to lay on someone with a traumatic brain injury.

"Everything's going along as usual and then all shit breaks loose," one said.

The injured man made no response, nor could he, since he had a trach.

To Quintana's left lay a man from Massachusetts who had been in the hospital for several months. He and his wife had been in Los Angeles visiting their children, there had been a fall from a ladder, he had seemed all right. One more perfectly ordinary day. Then he had trouble speaking. *Everything's going along as usual and then all shit breaks loose.* Now he had pneumonia. The children came and went. The wife was always there, pleading with him in a low mournful voice. The husband made no response: he too had a trach.

They did the trach for Quintana on the first of April, a Thursday afternoon.

By Friday morning enough of the sedation for the breathing tube had been metabolized out that she could open her eyes and squeeze my hand.

On Saturday I was told that the next day or Monday she would be moved from the ICU into a step-down neuro-observational unit on the seventh floor. The sixth and seventh floors at UCLA were all neuro.

I have no memory of when she was moved but I think it was some days after that.

One afternoon after she had been moved to the step-down unit I ran into the woman from Massachusetts in the Café Med courtyard.

Her husband too had left the ICU, and was moving now to what she called a "subacute rehab facility." We each knew that "subacute rehab facilities" were what medical insurance carriers and hospital discharge coordinators called nursing homes but this went unmentioned. She had wanted him moved to the eleven-bed acute rehab unit at UCLA Neuropsychiatric but he had not been accepted. That was the phrase she used, "not been accepted." She was concerned about how she would get to the subacute facility—one of the two with an available bed was near LAX, the other in Chinatown—because she did not drive. The children had jobs, important jobs, they could not always be driving her.

We sat in the sun.

I listened. She asked about my daughter.

I did not want to tell her that my daughter would be moving to the eleven-bed acute rehab unit at Neuropsychiatric.

At some point I noticed that I was trying like a sheepdog to herd the doctors, pointing out edema to one intern, reminding another to obtain a urine culture to check out the blood in the Foley catheter line, insisting on a Doppler ultrasound to see if the reason for the leg pain could be emboli, doggedly repeating—when the ultrasound indicated that she was in fact again throwing clots—that I wanted a specialist on coagulation called in to consult. I wrote down the name of the specialist I wanted. I offered to call him myself. These efforts did not endear me to the young men and women who made up the house staff ("If you want to manage this case I'm signing off," one finally said) but they made me feel less helpless.

I remember learning at UCLA the names of many tests and scales. The Kimura Box Test. The Two-Point Discrimination Test. The Glasgow Coma Scale, the Glasgow Outcome Scale. My comprehension of the meaning of these tests and scales remained obscure. I also remember learning, both at UCLA and before, at Beth Israel and Columbia-Presbyterian, the names of many resistant hospital bacteria. At Beth Israel there had been *Acinetobacter baumannii,* which was resistant to vancomycin. "That's how you know it's a hospital infection," I recall being told by a doctor I asked at Columbia-

Presbyterian. "If it's resistant to vanc it's hospital. Because vanc only gets used in hospital settings." At UCLA there had been MRSA, methicillin-resistant *Staphylococcus aureus*, as opposed to MRSE, methicillin-resistant *Staphylococcus epidermidis*, which was what they first thought they had cultured and which had seemed to more visibly alarm the staff. "I can't say why but since you're pregnant you may want to transfer off," one therapist advised another during the MRSE scare, glancing at me as if I might not understand. There were many other names of hospital bacteria, but those were the big hitters. Whatever bacteria was shown to be the source of the new fever or urinary tract infection, it would mandate gowns, gloves, masks. It would provoke heavy sighing among the aides who were required to suit up before entering the room to empty a wastebasket. The methicillin-resistant *Staphylococcus aureus* at UCLA was an infection in the bloodstream, a bacteremia. When I heard this I expressed concern to the doctor who was examining Quintana that an infection in her bloodstream might again lead to sepsis.

"Well, you know, sepsis, it's a clinical term," the doctor said, then continued examining her.

I had pressed him.

"She's already in some degree of sepsis." He had seemed cheerful. "But we're continuing vanc. And so far her blood pressure is holding."

So. We were back to waiting to see if she lost blood pressure.

We were back to watching for septic shock.

Next we would be watching for ice floes on the East River.

In point of fact what I watched from the windows at UCLA was a swimming pool. I never once saw anyone swim in this swimming pool, although it was filled, filtered (I could see the little swirl where the water entered the filter and the bubbling where it reemerged), sparkling in the sun, and surrounded by patio tables, with parasols. One day when I was watching it I had a sharp memory of having gotten the idea to float candles and gardenias in the pool behind the house in Brentwood Park. We were having a party. It was an hour before the party but I was already dressed when the gardenia idea presented itself. I knelt on the coping and lit the candles and used the pool skimmer to guide the gardenias and candles into a random pattern. I stood up, pleased with the result. I put the pool skimmer away. When I glanced back at the pool, the gardenias had vanished and the candles were out, tiny drenched hulks bobbing furiously around the filter intake. They could not be sucked in because the filter was already clogged with gardenias. I spent the remaining forty-five minutes before the party cleaning the sodden gardenias from the filter and scooping out the candles and drying my dress with a hair dryer.

So far so good.

A memory of the house in Brentwood Park that involved neither John nor Quintana.

Unfortunately I thought of another. I had been alone in the kitchen of that house, late twilight, early evening, feeding the Bouvier we then had. Quintana was at Barnard. John was spending a few days at the apartment we had in New York. This would have been late 1987, the period during which he had begun talking about wanting us to spend more time in New York. I had discouraged this idea. Suddenly a red flashing light had filled the kitchen. I had gone to the window. There was an ambulance in front of a house across Marlboro Street, visible beyond the coral tree and two cords of stacked wood in our side yard. This was a neighborhood in which many houses, including the one across Marlboro Street, had side yards in which there were two cords of stacked wood. I had watched the house until the last light was gone and the ambulance left. The next morning when I was walking the Bouvier a neighbor told me what had happened. Two cords of stacked wood had not kept the woman in the house across Marlboro Street from becoming a widow at dinner.

I had called John in New York.

The red flashing light had by then seemed an urgent warning.

I said maybe he was right, we should spend more time in New York.

Watching the empty swimming pool from the window at

UCLA I could see the vortex coming but could not deflect it. The vortex in this instance would be the memory's insistent appointment-in-Samarra aspect. Had I not made that call would Quintana have moved back to Los Angeles when she graduated from Barnard? Had she been living in Los Angeles would Beth Israel North have happened, would Presbyterian have happened, would she be in UCLA today? Had I not misread the meaning of the red flashing light in late 1987 would I be able to get in my car today and drive west on San Vicente and find John at the house in Brentwood Park? Standing in the pool? Rereading *Sophie's Choice*?

Would I need to relive every mistake? If by accident I remembered the morning we drove down to St.-Tropez from Tony Richardson's house in the hills and had coffee on the street and bought the fish for dinner would I also need to remember the night I refused to swim in the moonlight because the Mediterranean was polluted and I had a cut on my leg? If I remembered the gamecock at Portuguese Bend would I also need to remember the long drive home from dinner to that house, and how many nights as we passed the refineries on the San Diego Freeway one or the other of us had said the wrong thing?

Or stopped speaking? Or imagined that the other had stopped speaking? "Each single one of the memories and expectations in which the libido is bound to the object is brought up and hypercathected, and detachment of the libido is accomplished in respect of it. . . . It is remarkable that this painful unpleasure is taken as a matter of course by us." So Freud explained what he saw as the "work" of grief, which as described sounded suspiciously like the vortex.

In point of fact the house in Brentwood Park from which I had seen the red flashing light and thought to evade it by moving to New York no longer existed. It was torn down to the ground and replaced (by a house marginally larger) a year after we sold it. The day we happened to be in Los Angeles and drove past the corner of Chadbourne and Marlboro and saw nothing left standing except the one chimney that allowed a tax advantage, I remembered the real estate agent telling me how meaningful it would be to the buyers were we to give them suitably inscribed copies of the books we had written in the house. We had done this. *Quintana and Friends, Dutch Shea, Jr.,* and *The Red White and Blue* for John, *Salvador, Democracy,* and *Miami* for me. When we saw the flattened lot from

the car, Quintana, in the back seat, burst into tears. My
first reaction was fury. I wanted the books back.

Did this corrective line of thinking stop the vortex?

Not hardly.

One morning when Quintana was still in the step-
down unit because the persistence of her fever necessi-
tated an echocardiogram to rule out endocarditis she
lifted her right hand for the first time. This was significant because it was on the right side of her body that the
effects of the trauma could be seen. Movement meant
that the traumatized nerves remained alive. Later that
day she kept wanting to get out of bed, and fell into a sulk
like a child when I said I would not help her. My memory
of that day is not at all mudgy.

It was decided in late April that sufficient time had
passed since the surgery to allow her to fly to New York.
The issue until then had been pressurization and the potential it presented for swelling. She would need trained
personnel to accompany her. A commercial flight was
ruled out. Arrangements were made to medevac her: an
ambulance from UCLA to an airport, an air ambulance to
Teterboro, and an ambulance from Teterboro to New York
University Hospital, where she would do neuro-rehab at

the Rusk Institute. Many conversations were held between UCLA and Rusk. Many records were faxed. A CD-
ROM of CT scans was prepared. A date was set for what
even I was now calling "the transfer": Thursday, April
29. Early that Thursday morning as I was about to check
out of the Beverly Wilshire I got a call from somewhere in
Colorado. The flight had been delayed. The plane was in
Tucson, where it had landed with "mechanical difficul-
ties." The mechanics in Tucson would look at it when
they came in, at ten mountain time. By early afternoon
Pacific time it was clear that the plane would not be flying. Another plane would be available the next morning,
but the next morning was a Friday, and UCLA did not
like to transfer on Fridays. At the hospital I pressed the
discharge coordinator to agree to the Friday transfer.

To delay the transfer into the following week could
only dispirit and confuse Quintana, I said, sure of my
ground.

Rusk had no problem with a Friday night admission, I
said, less sure.

There was nowhere I could stay over the weekend, I
lied.

By the time the discharge coordinator had agreed to
the Friday transfer Quintana was asleep. I sat for a while
in the sun on the plaza outside the hospital and watched
a helicopter circling to land on the roof. Helicopters were
always landing on the roof at UCLA, suggesting trauma

all over Southern California, remote scenes of highway carnage, distant falling cranes, bad days ahead for the husband or wife or mother or father who had not yet (even as the helicopter landed and the trauma team rushed the stretcher into triage) gotten the call. I remembered a summer day in 1970 when John and I stopped for a red light on St. Charles Avenue in New Orleans and noticed the driver of the next car suddenly slump over his steering wheel. His horn sounded. Several pedestrians ran up. A police officer materialized. The light changed, we drove on. John had been unable to get this image out of his mind. There he was, he had kept saying later. He was alive and then he was dead and we were watching. We saw him at the instant it happened. We knew he was dead before his family did.

Just an ordinary day.

"And then—gone."

The day of the flight, when it came, had seemed to unfold with the nonsequential inexorability of a dream. When I turned on the news in the early morning there was a guerrilla action on the freeways, truckers protesting the price of gasoline. Huge semi trucks had been deliberately jackknifed and abandoned on Interstate 5. Witnesses reported that the first semis to stop had carried the TV crews. SUVs had been waiting to take the truckers themselves from the blocked freeway. The video as I watched it had seemed dislocatingly French, 1968.

"Avoid the 5 if you can," the newscaster advised, then warned that according to "sources" (presumably the same TV crews who were traveling with the truckers) the truckers would also block other freeways, specifically the 710, the 60, and the 10. In the normal course of this kind of disruption it would have seemed unlikely that we could get from UCLA to the plane, but by the time the ambulance arrived at the hospital the entire French event seemed to have dematerialized, that phase of the dream forgotten.

There were other phases to come. I had been told the plane would be at Santa Monica Airport. The ambulance crew had been told Burbank. Someone made a call and was told Van Nuys. When we reached Van Nuys there were no planes in sight, only helicopters. That must be because you're going by helicopter, one of the ambulance attendants said, clearly ready to hand us off and get on with his day. I don't think so, I said, it's three thousand miles. The ambulance attendant shrugged and disappeared. The plane was located, a jet Cessna with room for the two pilots, the two paramedics, the stretcher to which Quintana was strapped, and, if I sat on a bench over the oxygen canisters, me. We took off. We flew for a while. One of the paramedics had a digital camera and was taking pictures of what he kept referring to as the Grand Canyon. I said I believed it was Lake Mead, Hoover Dam. I pointed out Las Vegas.

The paramedic continued taking pictures.

He also continued referring to it as the Grand Canyon.

Why do you always have to be right, I remembered John saying.

It was a complaint, a charge, part of a fight.

He never understood that in my own mind I was never right. Once in 1971, when we were moving from Franklin Avenue to Malibu, I found a message stuck behind a picture I was taking down. The message was from someone to whom I had been close before I married John. He had spent a few weeks with us in the house on Franklin Avenue. This was the message: "You were wrong." I did not know what I had been wrong about but the possibilities seemed infinite. I burned the message. I never mentioned it to John.

All right it's the Grand Canyon, I thought, shifting position on the bench over the oxygen canisters so that I could no longer see out the window.

Later we landed in a cornfield in Kansas to refuel. The pilots struck a deal with the two teenagers who managed the airstrip: during the refueling they would take their pickup to a McDonald's and bring back hamburgers. While we waited the paramedics suggested that we take turns getting some exercise. When my turn came I stood frozen on the tarmac for a moment, ashamed to be free and outside when Quintana could not be, then walked to where the runway ended and the corn started. There was a little rain and unstable air and I imagined a tornado coming. Quintana and I were Dorothy. We were both free. In fact we were out of here. John had written a tornado into *Nothing Lost.* I remembered reading the last-pass galleys in Quintana's room at Presbyterian and crying when I hit the passage with the tornado. The protagonists, J.J. McClure and Teresa Kean, see the tornado "in the far distance, black and then milky when the sun caught it, moving like a huge reticulated vertical snake." J.J. tells Teresa not to worry, this stretch had been hit before, twisters never hit the same place twice.

> The tornado finally set down without incident just across the Wyoming line. That night in the Step Right Inn, at the junction between Higginson and Higgins, Teresa asked if it was true that tornadoes never hit the same place twice. "I don't know," J.J. said. "It seemed logical. Like lightning. You were worried. I didn't want you worried." It was as close a declaration of love as J.J. was capable of making.

Back in the plane, alone with Quintana, I took one of the hamburgers the teenagers had brought and tore it into pieces so that she and I could share. After a few bites she shook her head. She had been allowed solid food for only a week or so and could not eat more. There was still a feeding tube in place in case she could not eat at all.

"Am I going to make it," she asked then.

I chose to believe that she was asking if she would make it to New York.

"Definitely," I told her.

I'm here. You're safe.

Definitely she would be okay in California, I remembered telling her five weeks before.

That night when we arrived at the Rusk Institute Gerry and Tony were waiting outside to meet the ambulance. Gerry asked how the flight had been. I said that we had shared a Big Mac in a cornfield in Kansas. "It wasn't a Big Mac," Quintana said. "It was a Quarter Pounder."

It had seemed to me on the day in Quintana's room at Presbyterian when I read the final proof for *Nothing Lost* that there might be a grammatical error in the last sentence of the passage about J.J. McClure and Teresa Kean and the tornado. I never actually learned the rules of grammar, relying instead only on what sounded right, but there was something here that I was not sure sounded right. The sentence in the last-pass galleys read: "It was as close a declaration of love as J.J. was capable of making." I would have added a preposition: "It was as close *to* a declaration of love as J.J. was capable of making."

I sat by the window and watched the ice floes on the Hudson and thought about the sentence. *It was as close a declaration of love as J.J. was capable of making.* It was not the kind of sentence, if you had written it, you would want wrong, but neither was it the kind of sentence, if that was the way you had written it, you would want changed. How had he written it? What did he have in mind? How would he want it? The decision was left to me. Any choice I made could carry the potential for abandonment, even betrayal. That was one reason I was crying in Quintana's hospital room. When I got home that night I checked the previous galleys and manuscripts. The error, if it was an error, had been there from the beginning. I left it as it was.

Why do you always have to be right.

Why do you always have to have the last word.

For once in your life just let it go.

12.

The day on which Quintana and I flew east on the Cessna that refueled in the cornfield in Kansas was April 30, 2004. During May and June and the half of July that she spent at the Rusk Institute there was very little I could do for her. I could go down to East Thirty-fourth Street to see her in the late afternoons, and most afternoons I did, but she was in therapy from eight in the morning until four in the afternoon and exhausted by six-thirty or seven. She was medically stable. She could eat, the feeding tube was still in place but no longer necessary. She was beginning to regain movement in her right leg and arm. She was regaining the mobility in her right eye that she needed to read. On weekend days when she did not have therapy Gerry would take her to lunch and a movie in the neighborhood. He would eat dinner with her. Friends would join them for picnic lunches. For as long as she was at Rusk I could water the plants on her windowsill, I could find the marginally different sneakers her therapist had decreed, I could sit with her in the greenhouse off the Rusk lobby watching the koi in the pond, but once she left Rusk I would no longer be able to do even that. She was reaching a point at which she would need once again to be, if she was to recover, on her own.

I determined to spend the summer reaching the same point.

I did not yet have the concentration to work but I could straighten my house, I could get on top of things, I could deal with my unopened mail.

That I was only now beginning the process of mourning did not occur to me.

Until now I had been able only to grieve, not mourn. Grief was passive. Grief happened. Mourning, the act of dealing with grief, required attention. Until now there had been every urgent reason to obliterate any attention that might otherwise have been paid, banish the thought, bring fresh adrenaline to bear on the crisis of the day. I had passed an entire season during which the only words I allowed myself to truly hear were recorded: *Wel*-come to *U-C-L-A*.

I began.

Among the letters and books and magazines that had arrived while I was in Los Angeles was a thick volume called *Lives of '54*, prepared for what was by then the im-

minent fiftieth reunion of John's class at Princeton. I
looked up John's entry. It read: "William Faulkner once
said that a writer's obituary should read, 'He wrote books,
then he died.' This is not an obit (at least as of 19
September 2002) and I am still writing books. So I'll
stick with Faulkner."

I told myself: this was not an obit.

At least as of 19 September 2002.

I closed *Lives of '54*. A few weeks later I opened it
again, and leafed through the other entries. One was from
Donald H. ("Rummy") Rumsfeld, who noted: "After
Princeton, the years seem like a blur, but the days seem
more like rapid fire." I thought about this. Another, a
three-page reflection by Lancelot L. ("Lon") Farrar, Jr.,
began: "Arguably our best-shared Princeton memory was
Adlai Stevenson's address to the senior banquet."

I also thought about this.

I had been married to a member of the Class of '54
for forty years and he had never mentioned Adlai Stevenson's address to the senior banquet. I tried to think of
anything at all he had mentioned about Princeton. He
had many times mentioned the misguided entitlement he
heard in the words "Princeton in the Nation's Service,"
the slogan Princeton had adopted from a speech by
Woodrow Wilson. Other than that I could think of nothing except his saying a few days after our wedding (why
did he say it? how had it come up?) that he had thought
the Nassoons absurd. In fact, because he knew it amused

me, he would sometimes impersonate the Nassoons in performance: the studied plunge of one hand into a pocket, the swirling of the ice cubes in the imaginary glass, the chin thrust into profile, the slight satisfied smile.

> *As I remember you—*
> *You stood there beside me on a high windy slope—*
> *Our faces to the wind and our hearts full of hope—*

For forty years this song had figured in a private joke between us and I could not remember its name, let alone the rest of its lyrics. Finding the lyrics became a matter of some urgency. I could find only a single reference on the Internet, in an obituary from the *Princeton Alumni Weekly:*

John MacFadyen '46 *49: John MacFadyen died February 18, 2000, in Damariscotta, Maine, near the village of Head Tide, where he and his wife, Mary-Esther, made their home. The cause of death was pneumonia, but his health failed for some years, particularly after his wife's death in 1977. John came to Princeton from Duluth in the 'accelerated' summer of 1942. Gifted in music and arts, he contributed songs to Triangle, including, "As I Remember You," long a Nassoons favorite. John was the life of any party with a piano. Remembered was his rendition of "Shine, Little Glow Worm," played upside down from under the piano. After U.S. Army service in Japan, he returned to Princeton for a master's of fine arts in architecture. In the New York firm Harrison & Abramowitz, he designed a main United Nations building. John received the Rome Prize in architecture, and, newly wed to Mary-Esther Edge, spent 1952–53 at Rome's American Academy. His private architectural practice, noted especially for the design of the Wolf Trap Center for the Arts outside Washington, was interrupted by his service, during the 1960s, under Gov. Nelson Rockefeller, as executive director of the first state arts council. The class joins his children, Camilla, Luke, William, and John and three grandchildren in mourning the loss of one of our most unforgettable members.

"As I Remember You," long a Nassoons favorite.

But how about the death of Mary-Esther?

And how long ago was it when the life of any party last played "Shine, Little Glow Worm" upside down from under the piano?

What would I give to be able to discuss this with John?

What would I give to be able to discuss anything at all with John? What would I give to be able to say one small thing that made him happy? What would that one small thing be? If I had said it in time would it have worked?

A night or two before he died John asked me if I was aware how many characters died in the novel he had just sent to press, *Nothing Lost*. He had been sitting in his office making a list of them. I added one he had overlooked. Some months after he died I picked up a legal pad on his desk to make a note. On the legal pad, in very faint pencil, his handwriting, was the list. It read:

> *Teresa Kean*
> *Parlance*
> *Emmett McClure*
> *Jack Broderick*
> *Maurice Dodd*
> *Four people in car*
> *Charlie Buckles*
> *Percy—electric chair (Percy Darrow)*
> *Walden McClure*

Why was the pencil so faint, I wondered.
Why would he use a pencil that barely left a mark.
When did he begin seeing himself as dead?
"It's not black and white," a young doctor at Cedars-Sinai Medical Center in Los Angeles had told me, in

1982, about the divide between life and death. We had been standing in an ICU at Cedars watching Nick and Lenny's daughter Dominique, who had the night before been strangled to the point of death. Dominique was lying there in the ICU as if she were asleep but she would not recover. She was breathing only on life support.

Dominique had been the four-year-old at John's and my wedding.

Dominique had been the cousin who supervised Quintana's parties and took her shopping for prom dresses and stayed with her if we were out of town. *Roses are red, violets are blue,* read the card on a glass of flowers Quintana and Dominique left on the kitchen table for our return from one such trip. *I wish you weren't home and Dominique does too. Love, Happy Mother's Day, D & Q.*

I remember thinking that the doctor was wrong. For as long as Dominique lay in this ICU she was alive. She could not keep herself alive unaided but she was alive. That was white. When they turned off the life support there would be a matter of some minutes before her systems shut down and then she would be dead. That was black.

There were no faint traces about dead, no pencil marks.

Any faint traces, any pencil marks, were left "a night or two before he died," or "a week or two before," in any case decisively *before he died.*

There was a divide.

The abrupt finality of this divide was something about which I thought a great deal during the late spring and summer after I came home from UCLA. A close friend, Carolyn Lelyveld, died in May, at Memorial Sloan-Kettering. Tony Dunne's wife, Rosemary Breslin, died in June, at Columbia-Presbyterian. In each of those cases the phrase "after long illness" would have seemed to apply, trailing its misleading suggestion of release, relief, resolution. In each of those long illnesses the possibility of death had been in the picture, in Carolyn's case for some months, in Rosemary's since 1989, when she was thirty-two. Yet having seen the picture in no way deflected, when it came, the swift empty loss of the actual event. It was still black and white. Each of them had been in the last instant alive, and then dead. I realized that I had never believed in the words I had learned as a child in order to be confirmed as an Episcopalian: *I believe in the Holy Ghost, the Holy Catholic Church, the Communion of Saints, the forgiveness of sins, the resurrection of the body, and the life everlasting, amen.*

I did not believe in the resurrection of the body.

Nor had Teresa Kean, Parlance, Emmett McClure, Jack Broderick, Maurice Dodd, the four people in the car, Charlie Buckles, Percy Darrow, or Walden McClure.

Nor had my Catholic husband.

I imagined this way of thinking to be clarifying, but in

point of fact it was so muddled as to contradict even itself.

I did not believe in the resurrection of the body but I
still believed that given the right circumstances he would
come back.

He who left the faint traces before he died, the
Number Three pencil.

One day it seemed important that I reread *Alcestis*. I had
last read it at sixteen or seventeen, for a paper on
Euripides, but recalled it as somehow relevant to this
question of the "divide." I remembered the Greeks in
general but *Alcestis* in particular as good on the passage
between life and death. They visualized it, they drama-
tized it, they made the dark water and the ferry into the
mise-en-scène itself. I did reread *Alcestis*. What happens
in the play is this: Admetus, the young king of Thessaly,
has been condemned by Death to die. Apollo has inter-
ceded, gaining a promise from the Fates that Admetus, if
he can find another mortal to die in his place, need not
die immediately. Admetus approaches his friends and
his parents, in vain. "I tell myself that we are a long time
underground and that life is short, but sweet," his father
tells him after declining to take his place.

Only the wife of Admetus, the young queen, Alcestis, volunteers. There is much wailing about her approaching death, but no one steps in to save her. She dies, at length: "I see the two-oared boat, / I see the boat on the lake! / And Charon, / Ferryman of the Dead, / Calls to me, his hand on the oar . . ." Admetus is overcome by guilt and shame and self-pity: "Alas! How bitter to me is that ferrying of which you speak! O my unhappy one, how we suffer!" He behaves in every way badly. He blames his parents. He insists that Alcestis is suffering less than he. After some pages (and quite enough) of this, Alcestis, by means of a remarkably (even for 430 B.C.) clumsy deus ex machina, is allowed to come back. She does not speak, but this is explained, again clumsily, as temporary, self-correcting: "You may not hear her voice until she is purified from her consecration to the Lower Gods, and until the third dawn is risen." If we rely on the text alone, the play ends happily.

This was not my memory of *Alcestis*, which suggests that I was already given, at sixteen or seventeen, to editing the text as I read it. The principal divergences between the text and my memory appear toward the end, when Alcestis returns from the dead. In my memory, the reason Alcestis does not speak is that she declines to speak. Admetus, as I remembered it, presses her, at which point, to his distress, since what she turns out to have on her mind are his revealed failings, she does

speak. Admetus, alarmed, shuts off the prospect of hearing more by calling for celebration. Alcestis acquiesces,
but remains remote, other. Alcestis is on the face of it
back with her husband and children, again the young
queen of Thessaly, but the ending ("my" ending) could
not be construed as happy.

In some ways this is a better (more "worked out") story,
one that at least acknowledges that death "changes" the
one who has died, but it opens up further questions about
the divide. If the dead were truly to come back, what
would they come back knowing? Could we face them?
We who allowed them to die? The clear light of day tells
me that I did not allow John to die, that I did not have
that power, but do I believe that? Does he?

Survivors look back and see omens, messages they
missed.

They remember the tree that died, the gull that splat-
tered onto the hood of the car.

They live by symbols. They read meaning into the bar-
rage of spam on the unused computer, the delete key that
stops working, the imagined abandonment in the decision to replace it. The voice on my answering machine is
still John's. The fact that it was his in the first place was

arbitrary, having to do with who was around on the day the answering machine last needed programming, but if I needed to retape it now I would do so with a sense of betrayal. One day when I was talking on the telephone in his office I mindlessly turned the pages of the dictionary that he had always left open on the table by the desk. When I realized what I had done I was stricken: what word had he last looked up, what had he been thinking? By turning the pages had I lost the message? Or had the message been lost before I touched the dictionary? Had I refused to hear the message?

I tell you that I shall not live two days, Gawain said.

Later in the summer I received another book from Princeton. It was a first edition copy of *True Confessions*, in, as the booksellers say, "good condition, original dust jacket slightly frayed." In fact it was John's own copy: he had apparently sent it to a classmate who was organizing, for the fiftieth reunion of the Class of 1954, an exhibition of books written by class members. "It occupied the position of honor," the classmate wrote to me, "since John was unquestionably the most distinguished writer in our class."

I studied the original dust jacket, slightly frayed, on the copy of *True Confessions*.

I remembered the first time I saw this jacket, or a mock-up of this jacket. It had sat around our house for days, as proposed designs and type samples and jackets for new books always did, the idea being to gauge whether or not it would wear well, continue to please the eye.

I opened the book. I looked at the dedication. "For Dorothy Burns Dunne, Joan Didion, Quintana Roo Dunne," the dedication read. "Generations."

I had forgotten this dedication. I had *not sufficiently appreciated it,* a persistent theme by that stage of whatever I was going through.

I reread *True Confessions.* I found it darker than I had remembered it. I reread *Harp.* I found a different, less sunny, version of the summer we watched *Tenko* and went to dinner at Morton's.

Something else had happened toward the end of that summer.

In August there had been a memorial service for an acquaintance (this was not in itself the "something else" that happened), a French tennis player in his sixties who had been killed in an accident. The memorial service had been on someone's court in Beverly Hills. "I met my wife at the service," John had written in *Harp,* "coming directly from a doctor's appointment in Santa Monica, and as I sat there under the hot August sun, death was very much on my mind. I thought Anton had actually died under the best possible circumstances for him, a moment of terror as he realized the inevitable outcome of the accident, then an instant later the eternal dark."

> The service ended and the parking attendant brought my car. As we drove away, my wife said, "What did the doctor say?"
>
> There had not been an appropriate moment to mention my visit to the doctor in Santa Monica. "He scared the shit out of me, babe."
>
> "What did he say?"
>
> "He said I was a candidate for a catastrophic cardiac event."

A few pages further in *Harp*, the writer, John, examines the veracity of this (his own) account. He notes a name changed, a certain dramatic restructuring, a minor time collapse. He asks himself: "Anything else?" This was the answer he gave: "When I told my wife he scared the shit out of me, I started to cry."

Either I had not remembered this or I had determinedly chosen not to remember this.

I had *not sufficiently appreciated it.*

Was that what he experienced as he himself died? "A moment of terror as he realized the inevitable outcome of the accident, then an instant later the eternal dark"? In the sense that it happens one night and not another, the mechanism of a typical cardiac arrest could be construed as essentially accidental: a sudden spasm ruptures a deposit of plaque in a coronary artery, ischemia follows, and the heart, deprived of oxygen, enters ventricular fibrillation.

But how did he experience it?

The "moment of terror," the "eternal dark"? Did he accurately intuit this when he was writing *Harp*? Did he, as we would say to each other to the point of whether something was accurately reported or perceived, "get it right"? What about the "eternal dark" part? Didn't the survivors of near-death experiences always mention "the white light"? It occurs to me as I write that this "white light," usually presented dippily (evidence of afterlife, higher power), is in fact precisely consistent with the oxygen deficit that occurs as blood flow to the brain decreases. "Everything went white," those whose blood pressure has dropped say of the instant before they faint. "All the color drained out," those bleeding internally report of the moment when blood loss goes critical.

The "something else" that happened toward the end of that summer, which must have been 1987, was the series of events that followed the appointment with the doctor in Santa Monica and the memorial service on the tennis court in Beverly Hills. A week or so later an angiogram was done. The angiogram showed a 90 percent occlusion of the left anterior descending artery, or LAD. It also showed a long 90 percent narrowing in the circumflex marginal artery, which was considered significant mainly because the circumflex marginal artery fed the same area of the heart as the occluded LAD. "We call it the widow-maker, pal," John's cardiologist in New York later said of the LAD. A week or two after the angiogram (it was by then September of that year, still summer in Los Angeles) an angioplasty was done. The results after two weeks, as demonstrated by an exercise echocardiogram, were said to be "spectacular." Another exercise echo after six months confirmed this success. Thallium scans over the next few years and a subsequent angiogram in 1991 gave the same confirmation. I recall that John and I took different views of what had happened in 1987. As he saw it, he now had a death sentence, temporarily suspended. He often said, after the 1987 angioplasty, that he now knew how he was going to die. As I saw it, the timing had been providential, the intervention successful, the problem solved, the mechanism fixed. You no more know how you're going to die than I do or anyone else does, I remember saying. I realize now that his was the more realistic view.

13.

I used to tell John my dreams, not to understand them but to get rid of them, clear my mind for the day. "Don't tell me your dream," he would say when I woke in the morning, but in the end he would listen.

When he died I stopped having dreams.

In the early summer I began to dream again, for the first time since it happened. Since I can no longer pass them off to John I find myself thinking about them. I remember a passage from a novel I wrote in the mid-1990s, *The Last Thing He Wanted:*

> Of course we would not need those last six notes to know what Elena's dreams were about.
>
> Elena's dreams were about dying.
>
> Elena's dreams were about getting old.
>
> Nobody here has not had (will not have) Elena's dreams.

We all know that.

The point is that Elena didn't.

The point is that Elena remained remote most of all to herself, a clandestine agent who had so successfully compartmentalized her operation as to have lost access to her own cutouts.

I realize that Elena's situation is my own.

In one dream I am hanging a braided belt in a closet when it breaks. About a third of the belt just drops off in my hands. I show the two pieces to John. I say (or he says, who knows in dreams) that this was his favorite belt. I determine (again, I think I determine, I should have determined, my half-waking mind tells me to do the right thing) to find him an identical braided belt.

In other words to fix what I broke, *bring him back.*

The similarity of this broken braided belt to the one I found in the plastic bag I was given at New York Hospital does not escape my attention. Nor does the fact that I am still thinking *I broke it, I did it, I am responsible.*

In another dream John and I are flying to Honolulu. Many other people are going, we have assembled at Santa Monica Airport. Paramount has arranged planes. Production assistants are distributing boarding passes. I board. There is confusion. Others are boarding but there is no sign of John. I worry that there is a problem with his boarding pass. I decide that I should leave the plane,

wait for him in the car. While I am waiting in the car I realize that the planes are taking off, one by one. Finally
there is no one but me on the tarmac. My first thought in
the dream is anger: John has boarded a plane without me.
My second thought transfers the anger: Paramount has
not cared enough about us to put us on the same plane.

What "Paramount" was doing in this dream would require another discussion, not relevant.

As I think about the dream I remember *Tenko. Tenko,*
as the series progresses, takes its imprisoned English-
women through their liberation from the Japanese camp
and their reunions in Singapore with their husbands,
which do not go uniformly well. There seemed for some a
level at which the husband was held responsible for the
ordeal of imprisonment. There seemed a sense, however
irrational, of having been abandoned. Did I feel abandoned, left behind on the tarmac, did I feel anger at John
for leaving me? Was it possible to feel anger and simultaneously to feel responsible?

I know the answer a psychiatrist would give to that
question.

The answer would have to do with the well-known way
in which anger creates guilt and vice versa.

I do not disbelieve this answer but it remains less sug-
gestive to me than the unexamined image, the mystery of
being left alone on the tarmac at Santa Monica Airport
watching the planes take off one by one.

We all know that.

The point is that Elena didn't.

I wake at what seems to be three-thirty in the morning and find a television set on, MSNBC. Either Joe Scarborough or Keith Olbermann is talking to a husband and wife, passengers on a flight from Detroit to Los Angeles, "Northwest 327" (I actually write this down, to tell to John), on which "a terrorist tryout" is said to have occurred. The incident seems to have involved fourteen men said to be "Arabs" who, at some point after takeoff from Detroit, began gathering outside the coach lavatory, entering one by one.

The couple now being interviewed on-screen reports having exchanged signals with the crew.

The plane landed in Los Angeles. The "Arabs," all fourteen of whom had "expired visas" (this seemed to strike MSNBC as more unusual than it struck me), were detained, then released. Everyone, including the couple on-screen, had gone about their day. It was not, then, "a terrorist attack," which seemed to be what made it "a terrorist tryout."

I need in the dream to discuss this with John.

Or was it even a dream?

Who is the director of dreams, would he care?

Was it only by dreaming or writing that I could find out what I thought?

When the twilights got long in June I forced myself to eat dinner in the living room, where the light was. After John died I had begun eating by myself in the kitchen (the dining room was too big and the table in the living room was where he had died), but when the long twilights came I had a strong sense that he would want me to see the light. As the twilights began to shorten I retreated again to the kitchen. I began spending more evenings alone at home. I was working, I would say. By the time August came I was in fact working, or trying to work, but I also wanted not to be out, exposed. One night I found myself taking from the cupboard not one of the plates I normally used but a crackled and worn Spode plate, from a set mostly broken or chipped, in a pattern no longer made, "Wickerdale." This had been a set of dishes, cream with a garland of small rose and blue flowers and ecru leaves, that John's mother had given him for the apartment he rented on East Seventy-third Street before we were married. John's mother was dead. John was dead. And I still had, of the "Wickerdale" Spode, four dinner plates, five salad plates, three butter plates, a single coffee cup, and nine saucers. I came to prefer these dishes to all others. By the end of the summer I was running the dishwasher a quarter full just to make sure that at least one of the four "Wickerdale" dinner plates would be clean when I needed it.

At a point during the summer it occurred to me that I had no letters from John, not one. We had only rarely been far or long apart. There had been the week or two or three here and there when one of us was doing a piece. There had been a month in 1975 when I taught at Berkeley during the week and flew home to Los Angeles on PSA every weekend. There had been a few weeks in 1988 when John was in Ireland doing research for *Harp* and I was in California covering the presidential primary. On all such occasions we had spoken on the telephone several times a day. We counted high telephone bills as part of our deal with each other, the same way we counted high bills for the hotels that enabled us to take Quintana out of school and fly somewhere and both work at the same time in the same suite. What I had instead of letters was a souvenir of one such hotel suite: a small black wafer-thin alarm clock he gave me one Christmas in Honolulu when we were doing a crash rewrite on a picture that never got made. It was one of those many Christmases on which we exchanged not "presents" but small practical things to make a tree. This alarm clock had stopped working during the year before he died, could not be repaired, and, after he died, could not be thrown out. It could not even be removed from the table by my bed. I also had a set of colored Buffalo pens, given to me the same Christmas, in the same spirit. I did many sketches of palm trees that Christmas, palm trees moving in the wind, palm trees dropping fronds, palm trees bent by the December *kona* storms. The colored Buffalo pens had long since gone dry, but, again, could not be thrown out.

I remember having had on that particular New Year's Eve in Honolulu a sense of well-being so profound that I did not want to go to sleep. We had ordered mahimahi and Manoa lettuce vinaigrette for the three of us from room service. We had tried for a festive effect by arranging leis over the printers and computers we were using for the rewrite. We had found candles and lit them and played the tapes Quintana had wrapped up to put under the tree. John had been reading on the bed and had fallen asleep about eleven-thirty. Quintana had gone downstairs to see what was happening. I could see John sleeping. I knew Quintana was safe, she had been going downstairs to see what was happening in this hotel (sometimes alone, sometimes with Susan Traylor, who often came along with Quintana when we were working in Honolulu) since she was six or seven years old. I sat on a balcony overlooking the Waialae Country Club golf course and finished the bottle of wine we had drunk with dinner and watched the neighborhood fireworks all over Honolulu.

I remember one last present from John. It was my birthday, December 5, 2003. Snow had begun falling in

New York around ten that morning and by evening seven inches had accumulated, with another six due. I remember snow avalanching off the slate roof at St. James' Church across the street. A plan to meet Quintana and Gerry at a restaurant was canceled. Before dinner John sat by the fire in the living room and read to me out loud. The book from which he read was a novel of my own, *A Book of Common Prayer,* which he happened to have in the living room because he was rereading it to see how something worked technically. The sequence he read out loud was one in which Charlotte Douglas's husband Leonard pays a visit to the narrator, Grace Strasser-Mendana, and lets her know that what is happening in the country her family runs will not end well. The sequence is complicated (this was in fact the sequence John had meant to reread to see how it worked technically), broken by other action and requiring the reader to pick up the undertext in what Leonard Douglas and Grace Strasser-Mendana say to each other. "Goddamn," John said to me when he closed the book. "Don't ever tell me again you can't write. That's my birthday present to you."

I remember tears coming to my eyes.

I feel them now.

In retrospect this had been my omen, my message, the early snowfall, the birthday present no one else could give me.

He had twenty-five nights left to live.

14.

There came a time in the summer when I began feeling fragile, unstable. A sandal would catch on a sidewalk and I would need to run a few steps to avoid the fall. What if I didn't? What if I fell? What would break, who would see the blood streaming down my leg, who would get the taxi, who would be with me in the emergency room? Who would be with me once I came home?

I stopped wearing sandals. I bought two pairs of Puma sneakers and wore them exclusively.

I started leaving lights on through the night. If the house was dark I could not get up to make a note or look for a book or check to make sure I had turned off the stove. If the house was dark I would lie there immobilized, entertaining visions of household peril, the books that could slide from the shelf and knock me down, the rug that could slip in the hallway, the washing machine hose that could have flooded the kitchen unseen in the dark, the better to electrocute whoever turned on a light to check the stove. That this was something more than prudent caution first came to my attention one afternoon when an acquaintance, a young writer, came by to ask if he could write a profile about me. I heard myself say, too urgent, that I could not possibly be written about. I was in no shape to be written about. I heard myself overstressing this, fighting to regain balance, avert the fall.

I thought about this later.

I realized that for the time being I could not trust myself to present a coherent face to the world.

Some days later I was stacking some copies of *Daedalus* that were lying around the house. Stacking magazines seemed at that point the limit of what I could do by way of organizing my life. Careful not to push this limit too far, I opened one of the copies of *Daedalus*. There was a story by Roxana Robinson, called "Blind Man." In this story, a man is driving in the rain at night to deliver a lecture. The reader picks up danger signals: the man cannot immediately recall the subject of his lecture, he takes his small rented car into the fast lane oblivious to an approaching SUV; there are references to someone, "Juliet," to whom something troubling has happened. Gradually we learn that Juliet was the man's daughter, who, on her first night alone after a college suspension and rehab and a restorative few weeks in the country with

her mother and father and sister, had done enough co-
caine to burst an artery in her brain and die.

One of the several levels on which the story disturbed
me (the most obvious being the burst artery in the child's
brain) was this: the father has been rendered fragile, unstable. The father is me.

In fact I know Roxana Robinson slightly. I think of
calling her. She knows something I am just beginning to
learn. But it would be unusual, intrusive, to call her: I
have met her only once, at a cocktail party on a roof.
Instead I think about people I know who have lost a husband or wife or child. I think particularly about how
these people looked when I saw them unexpectedly—on
the street, say, or entering a room—during the year or so
after the death. What struck me in each instance was
how exposed they seemed, how raw.

How fragile, I understand now.

How unstable.

I open another issue of *Daedalus,* this one devoted to
the concept of "happiness." One piece on happiness, the
joint work of Robert Biswas-Diener of the University of
Oregon and Ed Diener and Maya Tamir of the University
of Illinois, Champaign-Urbana, noted that although "research has shown that people can adapt to a wide range
of good and bad life events in less than two months,"
there remained "some events to which people are slow or
unable to adapt completely." Unemployment was one

such event. "We also find," the authors added, "that it
takes the average widow many years after her spouse's
death to regain her former level of life satisfaction."

Was I "the average widow"? What in fact would have
been my "former level of life satisfaction"?

I see a doctor, a routine follow-up. He asks how I am.
This should not be, in a doctor's office, an unforeseeable
question. Yet I find myself in sudden tears. This doctor is
a friend. John and I went to his wedding. He married the
daughter of friends who lived across the street from us in
Brentwood Park. The ceremony took place under their
jacaranda tree. In the first days after John died this doctor had come by the house. When Quintana was at Beth
Israel North he had gone up with me on a Sunday afternoon and talked to the doctors on the unit. When
Quintana was at Columbia-Presbyterian, his own hospital although she was not his patient, he had stopped in to
see her every evening. When Quintana was at UCLA and
he happened to be in California he had taken an afternoon to come by the neuroscience unit and talk to the
doctors there. He had talked to them and then he had
talked to the neuro people at Columbia and then he had
explained it all to me. He had been kind, helpful, encouraging, a true friend. In return I was crying in his office because he asked how I was.

"I just can't see the upside in this," I heard myself say
by way of explanation.

Later he said that if John had been sitting in the office he would have found this funny, as he himself had found it. "Of course I knew what you meant to say, and John would have known too, you meant to say you couldn't see the light at the end of the tunnel."

I agreed, but this was not in fact the case.

I had meant pretty much exactly what I said: I couldn't see the upside in this.

As I thought about the difference between the two sentences I realized that my impression of myself had been of someone who could look for, and find, the upside in any situation. I had believed in the logic of popular songs. I had looked for the silver lining. I had walked on through the storm. It occurs to me now that these were not even the songs of my generation. They were the songs, and the logic, of the generation or two that preceded my own. The score for my generation was Les Paul and Mary Ford, "How High the Moon," a different logic altogether. It also occurs to me, not an original thought but novel to me, that the logic of those earlier songs was based on self-pity. The singer of the song about looking for the silver lining believes that clouds have come her way. The singer of the song about walking on through the storm assumes that the storm could otherwise take her down.

I kept saying to myself that I had been lucky all my life. The point, as I saw it, was that this gave me no right to think of myself as unlucky now.

This was what passed for staying on top of the self-pity question.

I even believed it.

Only at a later point did I begin to wonder: what exactly did "luck" have to do with it? I could not on examination locate any actual instances of "luck" in my history. ("That was lucky," I once said to a doctor after a test revealed a soluble problem that would have been, untreated, less soluble. "I wouldn't call it lucky," she said, "I'd call it the game plan.") Nor did I believe that "bad luck" had killed John and struck Quintana. Once when she was still at the Westlake School for Girls, Quintana mentioned what she seemed to consider the inequable distribution of bad news. In the ninth grade she had come home from a retreat at Yosemite to learn that her uncle Stephen had committed suicide. In the eleventh grade she had been woken at Susan's at six-thirty in the morning to learn that Dominique had been murdered. "Most people I know at Westlake don't even know anyone who died," she said, "and just since I've

been there I've had a murder and a suicide in my
family."

"It all evens out in the end," John said, an answer that
bewildered me (what did it mean, couldn't he do better
than that?) but one that seemed to satisfy her.

Several years later, after Susan's mother and father
died within a year or two of each other, Susan asked if I
remembered John telling Quintana that it all evened out
in the end. I said I remembered.

"He was right," Susan said. "It did."

I recall being shocked. It had never occurred to me
that John meant that bad news will come to each of us.
Either Susan or Quintana had surely misunderstood. I
explained to Susan that John had meant something entirely different: he had meant that people who get bad
news will eventually get their share of good news.

"That's not what I meant at all," John said.

"I knew what he meant," Susan said.

Had I understood nothing?

Consider this matter of "luck."

Not only did I not believe that "bad luck" had killed
John and struck Quintana but in fact I believed precisely
the opposite: I believed that I should have been able to

prevent whatever happened. Only after the dream about being left on the tarmac at the Santa Monica Airport did it occur to me that there was a level on which I was not actually holding myself responsible. I was holding John and Quintana responsible, a significant difference but not one that took me anywhere I needed to be. *For once in your life just let it go.*

15.

A few months after John died, in the late winter of 2004, after Beth Israel and Presbyterian but before UCLA, I was asked by Robert Silvers at *The New York Review of Books* if I wanted him to submit my name for credentials to cover the Democratic and Republican summer conventions. I had looked at the dates: late July in Boston for the Democratic convention, the week before Labor Day in New York for the Republican convention. I had said yes. At the time it had seemed a way of committing to a normal life without needing actually to live it for another season or two, until spring had come and summer had come and fall was near.

Spring had come and gone, largely at UCLA.

In the middle of July Quintana was discharged from the Rusk Institute.

Ten days later I went to Boston for the Democratic convention. I had not anticipated that my new fragility would travel to Boston, a city devoid, I thought, of potentially tricky associations. I had been with Quintana in Boston only once, on a book tour. We had stayed at the Ritz. Her favorite stop on this tour had been Dallas. She had found Boston "all white." "You mean you didn't see many black people in Boston," Susan Traylor's mother had said when Quintana got back to Malibu and reported on her trip. "No," Quintana had said. "I mean it's not in color." The last several times I had needed to be in Boston I had gone alone, and in each case arranged the day so as to get the last shuttle back; the single time I could remember being there with John was for a preview of *True Confessions,* and all I remembered of that was having lunch at the Ritz and walking with John to Brooks Brothers to pick up a shirt and hearing, after the picture was shown and the response evaluated, this disheartening assessment of its commercial prospects: *True Confessions* could do very well, the market researcher said, among adults with sixteen-plus years of education.

I would not be staying at the Ritz.

There would be no need to go to Brooks Brothers.

There would be market researchers, but what bad news they delivered would not be mine.

I did not realize that there was still room for error until I was walking to the Fleet Center for the opening of the convention and found myself in tears. The first day of the Democratic convention was July 26, 2004. The day of

Quintana's wedding had been July 26, 2003. Even as I waited in the security line, even as I picked up releases in the press center, even as I located my seat and stood for the national anthem, even as I bought a hamburger at the McDonald's in the Fleet Center and sat on the lowest step of a barricaded stairway to eat it, the details sprang back. "In another world" was the phrase that would not leave my mind. Quintana sitting in the sunlight in the living room having her hair braided. John asking me which of two ties I preferred. Opening the boxes of flowers on the grass outside the cathedral and shaking the water off the leis. John giving a toast before Quintana cut the cake. The pleasure he took in the day and the party and her transparent happiness. "More than one more day," he had whispered to her before he walked her to the altar.

"More than one more day," he had whispered to her on the five days and nights he saw her in the Beth Israel North ICU.

"More than one more day," I had whispered to her in his absence on the days and nights that followed.

As you used to say to me, she had said when she stood in her black dress at St. John the Divine on the day we committed his ashes.

I recall being seized by the overwhelming conviction that I needed to get out of the Fleet Center, now. I have only rarely experienced panic but what set in next was recognizably panic. I remember trying to calm myself by seeing it as a Hitchcock movie, every shot planned to terrify but ultimately artifice, a game. There was the proximity of my assigned section to the netting that held the balloons for the balloon drop. There were the shadowy silhouettes moving on the high catwalks. There was the steam or smoke leaking from a vent over the sky boxes. There were, once I fled my seat, the corridors that seemed to go nowhere, mysteriously emptied, the walls slanted and distorted (the Hitchcock movie I was seeing would have to be *Spellbound*) ahead of me. There were the immobilized escalators. There were the elevators that did not respond to the push of the button. There were, once I managed to get downstairs, the empty commuter trains frozen in place beyond the locked glass wall (again, slanted and distorted as I approached it) that opened to the North Station tracks.

I got out of the Fleet Center.

I watched the end of that night's session on television in my room at the Parker House. There had seemed about this room at the Parker House when I first walked into it the day before something déjà vu, which I had put from my mind. Only now, as I was watching C-SPAN and listening to the air conditioner cycle on and off on its own schedule, did I remember: I had stayed in just such a room at the Parker House for a few nights between my junior and senior years at Berkeley. I had been in New

York for a college promotion *Mademoiselle* then ran (the "Guest Editor" program, memorialized by Sylvia Plath in *The Bell Jar*) and was returning to California via Boston and Quebec, an "educational" itinerary arranged, in retrospect dreamily, by my mother. The air conditioner had been cycling on and off on its own schedule even in 1955. I could remember sleeping until afternoon, miserable, then taking a subway to Cambridge, where I must have walked around aimlessly and taken the subway back.

These shards from 1955 were coming to me in such shredded (or "spotty," or even "mudgy") form (what did I do in Cambridge, what possibly could I have done in Cambridge?) that I had trouble holding them, but I tried, because for so long as I was thinking about the summer of 1955 I would not be thinking about John or Quintana.

In the summer of 1955 I had taken a train from New York to Boston.

In the summer of 1955 I had taken another train from Boston to Quebec. I stayed in a room at the Château Frontenac that did not have its own bathtub.

Did mothers always try to press on their daughters the itineraries of which they themselves had dreamed?

Did I?

This was not working.

I tried going further back, earlier than 1955, to Sacramento, high school dances at Christmastime. This felt safe. I thought about the way we danced, close. I thought about the places on the river we went after the dances. I thought about the fog on the levee driving home.

I fell asleep maintaining focus on the fog on the levee.

I woke at four a.m. The point about the fog on the levee was that you couldn't see the white line, someone had to walk ahead to guide the driver. Unfortunately there had been another place in my life where the fog got so thick that I had to walk ahead of the car.

The house on the Palos Verdes Peninsula.

The one to which we brought Quintana when she was three days old.

When you came off the Harbor Freeway and through San Pedro and onto the drive above the sea you hit the fog.

You (I) got out of the car to walk the white line.

The driver of the car was John.

I did not risk waiting for the panic to follow. I got a taxi to Logan. I avoided looking, as I bought a coffee at the Starbucks franchise outside the Delta shuttle, at its decorative garland of red-white-and-blue foil strips, presumably conceived as a festive "convention" touch but instead glittering forlornly, Christmas in the tropics. *Mele Kalikimaka.* Merry Christmas in Hawaiian. The little black alarm clock I could not throw away. The dried-out Buffalo pens I could not throw away. On the flight to LaGuardia I remember thinking that the most beautiful things I had ever seen had all been seen from airplanes.

The way the American west opens up. The way in which, on a polar flight across the Arctic, the islands in the sea give way imperceptibly to lakes on the land. The sea between Greece and Cyprus in the morning. The Alps on the way to Milan. I saw all those things with John.

How could I go back to Paris without him, how could I go back to Milan, Honolulu, Bogotá?

I couldn't even go to Boston.

A week or so before the Democratic convention, Dennis Overbye of *The New York Times* had reported a story involving Stephen W. Hawking. At a conference in Dublin, according to the *Times,* Dr. Hawking said that he had been wrong thirty years before when he asserted that information swallowed by a black hole could never be retrieved from it. This change of mind was "of great consequence to science," according to the *Times,* "because if Dr. Hawking had been right, it would have violated a basic tenet of modern physics: that it is always possible to reverse time, run the proverbial film backward and reconstruct what happened in, say, the collision of two cars or the collapse of a dead star into a black hole."

I had clipped this story, and carried it with me to Boston.

Something in the story seemed urgent to me, but I did not know what it was until a month later, the first afternoon of the Republican convention in Madison Square Garden. I was on the Tower C escalator. The last time I had been on such an escalator in the Garden was with John, in November, the night before we flew to Paris. We had gone with David and Jean Halberstam to see the Lakers play the Knicks. David had gotten seats through the commissioner of the NBA, David Stern. The Lakers won. Rain had been sluicing down the glass beyond the escalator. "It's good luck, an omen, a great way to start this trip," I remembered John saying. He did not mean the good seats and he did not mean the Laker win and he did not mean the rain, he meant we were doing something we did not ordinarily do, which had become an issue with him. We were not having any fun, he had recently begun pointing out. I would take exception (didn't we do this, didn't we do that) but I had also known what he meant. He meant doing things not because we were expected to do them or had always done them or should do them but because we wanted to do them. He meant wanting. He meant living.

This trip to Paris was the one over which we had fought.

This trip to Paris was the one he said he needed to take because otherwise he would never see Paris again.

I was still on the Tower C escalator.

Another vortex revealed itself.

The last time I covered a convention at Madison Square Garden had been 1992, the Democratic convention.

John would wait until I came uptown at eleven or so to have dinner with me. We would walk to Coco Pazzo on those hot July nights and split an order of pasta and a salad at one of the little unreserved tables in the bar. I do not think we ever discussed the convention during these late dinners. On the Sunday afternoon before it began I had talked him into going uptown with me to a Louis Farrakhan event that never materialized, and between the improvisational nature of the scheduling and the walk back downtown from 125th Street his tolerance for the 1992 Democratic convention was pretty much exhausted.

Still.

He waited every night to eat with me.

I thought about all this on the Tower C escalator and suddenly it occurred to me: I had spent a minute or two on this escalator thinking about the November night in 2003 before we flew to Paris and about those July nights in 1992 when we would eat late at Coco Pazzo and about the afternoon we had stood around 125th Street waiting for the Louis Farrakhan event that never happened. I had stood on this escalator thinking about those days and nights without once thinking I could change their outcome. I realized that since the last morning of 2003, the morning after he died, I had been trying to reverse time, run the film backward.

It was now eight months later, August 30, 2004, and I still was.

The difference was that all through those eight months I had been trying to substitute an alternate reel. Now I was trying only to reconstruct the collision, the collapse of the dead star.

16.

I said I knew what John meant when he said we were not having any fun.

What he meant was something that had to do with Joe and Gertrude Black, a couple we had met in Indonesia in December 1980. We were there on a USIA trip, giving lectures and meeting Indonesian writers and academics. The Blacks had shown up in a classroom one morning at Gadjah Mada University in Jogjakarta, an American couple apparently at home in the remote and in many ways alien tropic of central Java, their faces open and strikingly luminous. "The critical theories of Mr. I. A. Richards," I remember a student asking me that morning. "What think?" Joe Black was then in his fifties, Gertrude a year or two younger but again, I suppose in her fifties. He had retired from the Rockefeller Foundation and come to Jogjakarta to teach political science at Gadjah Mada. He had grown up in Utah. As a young man he

had been an extra in John Ford's *Fort Apache*. He and
Gertrude had four children, one of whom had been, he
said, hit hard by the 1960s. We talked to the Blacks only
twice, once at Gadjah Mada and a day later at the airport,
when they came to see us off, but each of these conversations was curiously open, as if we had found ourselves
stranded together on an island. Over the years John mentioned Joe and Gertrude Black frequently, in each case
as exemplary, what he thought of as the best kind of
American. They represented something personal to him.
They were models for the life he wanted us eventually
to live. Because he had mentioned them again a few
days before he died I searched his computer for their
names. I found the names in a file called "AAA Random
Thoughts," one of the files in which he kept notes for the
book he was trying to get off the ground. The note after
their names was cryptic: "Joe and Gertrude Black: The
concept of service."

I knew what he meant by that too.

He had wanted to be Joe and Gertrude Black. So had I.
We hadn't made it. "Fritter away" was a definition in the
crossword that morning. The word it defined was five letters, "waste." Was that what we had done? Was that what
he thought we had done?

Why didn't I listen when he said we weren't having
any fun?

Why didn't I move to change our life?

According to the computer dating the file called "AAA Random Thoughts" was last amended at 1:08 p.m. on December 30, 2003, the day of his death, six minutes after I saved the file that ended *how does "flu" morph into whole-body infection.* He would have been in his office and I would have been in mine. I cannot stop where this leads me. We should have been together. Not necessarily in a classroom in central Java (I do not have a sufficiently deluded view of either of us to see that scenario intact, nor was a classroom in central Java what he meant) but together. The file called "AAA Random Thoughts" was eighty pages long. What it was he added or amended and saved at 1:08 p.m. that afternoon I have no way of knowing.

17.

Grief turns out to be a place none of us know until we reach it. We anticipate (we know) that someone close to us could die, but we do not look beyond the few days or weeks that immediately follow such an imagined death. We misconstrue the nature of even those few days or weeks. We might expect if the death is sudden to feel shock. We do not expect this shock to be obliterative, dislocating to both body and mind. We might expect that we will be prostrate, inconsolable, crazy with loss. We do not expect to be literally crazy, cool customers who believe that their husband is about to return and need his shoes. In the version of grief we imagine, the model will be "healing." A certain forward movement will prevail. The worst days will be the earliest days. We imagine that the moment to most severely test us will be the funeral, after which this hypothetical healing will take place. When we anticipate the funeral we wonder about failing to "get through it," rise to the occasion, exhibit the "strength" that invariably gets mentioned as the correct response to death. We anticipate needing to steel ourselves for the moment: will I be able to greet people, will I be able to leave the scene, will I be able even to get dressed that day? We have no way of knowing that this will not be the issue. We have no way of knowing that the funeral itself will be anodyne, a kind of narcotic regression in which we are wrapped in the care of others and the gravity and meaning of the occasion. Nor can we know ahead of the fact (and here lies the heart of the difference between grief as we imagine it and grief as it is) the unending absence that follows, the void, the very opposite of meaning, the relentless succession of moments during which we will confront the experience of meaninglessness itself.

As a child I thought a great deal about meaninglessness, which seemed at the time the most prominent negative feature on the horizon. After a few years of failing to find meaning in the more commonly recommended venues I learned that I could find it in geology, so I did. This in turn enabled me to find meaning in the Episcopal litany, most acutely in the words *as it was in the beginning, is*

now and ever shall be, world without end, which I interpreted as a literal description of the constant changing of
the earth, the unending erosion of the shores and mountains, the inexorable shifting of the geological structures
that could throw up mountains and islands and could just
as reliably take them away. I found earthquakes, even
when I was in them, deeply satisfying, abruptly revealed
evidence of the scheme in action. That the scheme could
destroy the works of man might be a personal regret but
remained, in the larger picture I had come to recognize, a
matter of abiding indifference. No eye was on the sparrow. No one was watching me. *As it was in the beginning,
is now and ever shall be, world without end.* On the day it
was announced that the atomic bomb had been dropped
on Hiroshima those were the words that came immediately to my ten-year-old mind. When I heard a few years
later about mushroom clouds over the Nevada test site
those were again the words that came to mind. I began
waking before dawn, imagining that the fireballs from the
Nevada test shots would light up the sky in Sacramento.

Later, after I married and had a child, I learned to find
equal meaning in the repeated rituals of domestic life.
Setting the table. Lighting the candles. Building the fire.
Cooking. All those soufflés, all that crème caramel, all
those daubes and albóndigas and gumbos. Clean sheets,
stacks of clean towels, hurricane lamps for storms,
enough water and food to see us through whatever geological event came our way. *These fragments I have shored*

against my ruins, were the words that came to mind then. These fragments mattered to me. I believed in them. That I could find meaning in the intensely personal nature of my life as a wife and mother did not seem inconsistent with finding meaning in the vast indifference of geology and the test shots; the two systems existed for me on parallel tracks that occasionally converged, notably during earthquakes. In my unexamined mind there was always a point, John's and my death, at which the tracks would converge for a final time. On the Internet I recently found aerial photographs of the house on the Palos Verdes Peninsula in which we had lived when we were first married, the house to which we had brought Quintana home from St. John's Hospital in Santa Monica and put her in her bassinet by the wisteria in the box garden. The photographs, part of the California Coastal Records Project, the point of which was to document the entire California coastline, were hard to read conclusively, but the house as it had been when we lived in it appeared to be gone. The tower where the gate had been seemed intact but the rest of the structure looked unfamiliar. There seemed to be a swimming pool where the wisteria and box garden had been. The area itself was identified as "Portuguese Bend landslide." You could see the slumping of the hill where the slide had occurred. You could also see, at the base of the cliff on the point, the cave into which we used to swim when the tide was at exactly the right flow.

The swell of clear water.

That was one way my two systems could have converged.

We could have been swimming into the cave with the swell of clear water and the entire point could have slumped, slipped into the sea around us. The entire point slipping into the sea around us was the kind of conclusion I anticipated. I did not anticipate cardiac arrest at the dinner table.

You sit down to dinner and life as you know it ends.
The question of self-pity.

People in grief think a great deal about self-pity. We worry it, dread it, scourge our thinking for signs of it. We fear that our actions will reveal the condition tellingly described as "dwelling on it." We understand the aversion most of us have to "dwelling on it." Visible mourning reminds us of death, which is construed as unnatural, a failure to manage the situation. "A single person is missing for you, and the whole world is empty," Philippe Ariès wrote to the point of this aversion in *Western Attitudes toward Death.* "But one no longer has the right to say so aloud." We remind ourselves repeatedly that our own loss is nothing compared to the loss experienced (or, the even worse thought, not experienced) by he or she who died; this attempt at corrective thinking serves only to plunge us deeper into the self-regarding deep. *(Why didn't I see that, why am I so selfish.)* The very language we use when we think about self-pity betrays the deep abhorrence in which we hold it: self-pity is *feeling sorry for yourself,* self-pity is *thumb-sucking,* self-pity is *boo hoo poor me,* self-pity is the condition in which those feeling sorry for themselves *indulge,* or even *wallow.* Self-pity remains both the most common and the most universally reviled of our character defects, its pestilential destructiveness accepted as given. "Our worst enemy," Helen Keller called it. *I never saw a wild thing / sorry for itself,* D. H. Lawrence wrote, in a much-quoted four-line homily that turns out on examination to be free of any but tendentious meaning. *A small bird will drop frozen dead from a bough / without ever having felt sorry for itself.*

This may be what Lawrence (or we) would prefer to believe about wild things, but consider those dolphins who refuse to eat after the death of a mate. Consider those geese who search for the lost mate until they themselves become disoriented and die. In fact the grieving have urgent reasons, even an urgent need, to feel sorry for themselves. Husbands walk out, wives walk out, divorces happen, but these husbands and wives leave behind them webs of intact associations, however acrimonious. Only the survivors of a death are truly left alone. The connections that made up their life—both the deep con-

nections and the apparently (until they are broken) in-
significant connections—have all vanished. John and I
were married for forty years. During all but the first five
months of our marriage, when John was still working at
Time, we both worked at home. We were together twenty-
four hours a day, a fact that remained a source of both
merriment and foreboding to my mother and aunts. "For
richer for poorer but never for lunch," one or another of
them frequently said in the early years of our marriage. I
could not count the times during the average day when
something would come up that I needed to tell him. This
impulse did not end with his death. What ended was the
possibility of response. I read something in the paper that
I would normally have read to him. I notice some change
in the neighborhood that would interest him: Ralph
Lauren has expanded into more space between Seventy-
first and Seventy-second Streets, say, or the empty space
where the Madison Avenue Bookshop used to be has finally been leased. I recall coming in from Central Park
one morning in mid-August with urgent news to report:
the deep summer green has faded overnight from the
trees, the season is already changing. *We need to make a
plan for the fall,* I remember thinking. *We need to decide
where we want to be at Thanksgiving, Christmas, the end
of the year.*

I am dropping my keys on the table inside the door
before I fully remember. There is no one to hear this

news, nowhere to go with the unmade plan, the uncompleted thought. There is no one to agree, disagree, talk back. "I think I am beginning to understand why grief feels like suspense," C. S. Lewis wrote after the death of his wife. "It comes from the frustration of so many impulses that had become habitual. Thought after thought, feeling after feeling, action after action, had H. for their object. Now their target is gone. I keep on through habit fitting an arrow to the string, then I remember and have to lay the bow down. So many roads lead thought to H. I set out on one of them. But now there's an impassable frontierpost across it. So many roads once; now so many cul de sacs."

We are repeatedly left, in other words, with no further focus than ourselves, a source from which self-pity naturally flows. Each time this happens (it happens still) I am struck again by the permanent impassibility of the divide. Some people who have lost a husband or wife report feeling that person's presence, receiving that person's advice. Some report actual sightings, what Freud described in "Mourning and Melancholia" as "a clinging to the object through the medium of a hallucinatory wishful psychosis." Others describe not a visible apparition but just a "very strongly felt presence." I experienced neither. There have been a few occasions (the day they wanted to do the trach at UCLA, for example) on which I asked John point blank what to do. I said I needed his help. I said I could not do this alone. I said these things out loud, actually vocalized the words.

I am a writer. Imagining what someone would say or do comes to me as naturally as breathing.

Yet on each occasion these pleas for his presence served only to reinforce my awareness of the final silence that separated us. Any answer he gave could exist only in my imagination, my edit. For me to imagine what he could say only in my edit would seem obscene, a violation. I could no more know what he would say about UCLA and the trach than I could know whether he meant to leave the "to" out of the sentence about J.J. McClure and Teresa Kean and the tornado. We imagined we knew everything the other thought, even when we did not necessarily want to know it, but in fact, I have come to see, we knew not the smallest fraction of what there was to know.

W*hen something happens to me,* he would frequently say.

Nothing will happen to you, I would say.

But if it does.

If it does, he would continue. If it did, for example, I was not to move to a smaller apartment. If it did I would be surrounded by people. If it did I would need to make plans to feed these people. If it did I would marry again within the year.

You don't understand, I would say.

And in fact he did not. Nor did I: we were equally incapable of imagining the reality of life without the other. This will not be a story in which the death of the husband or wife becomes what amounts to the credit sequence for a new life, a catalyst for the discovery that (a point typically introduced in such accounts by the precocious child of the bereaved) "you can love more than one person." Of course you can, but marriage is something different. Marriage is memory, marriage is time. "She didn't know the songs," I recall being told that a friend of a friend had said after an attempt to repeat the experience. Marriage is not only time: it is also, parodoxically, the denial of time. For forty years I saw myself through John's eyes. I did not age. This year for the first time since I was twenty-nine I saw myself through the eyes of others. This year for the first time since I was twenty-nine I realized that my image of myself was of someone significantly younger. This year I realized that one reason I was so often sideswiped by memories of Quintana at three was this: when Quintana was three I was thirty-four. I remember Gerard Manley Hopkins: *Margaret, are you grieving / Over Goldengrove unleaving?* and *It is the blight man was born for, / It is Margaret you mourn for.*

It is the blight *man* was born for.

We are not idealized wild things.

We are imperfect mortal beings, aware of that mortality even as we push it away, failed by our very complication, so wired that when we mourn our losses we also mourn, for better or for worse, ourselves. As we were. As we are no longer. As we will one day not be at all.

Elena's dreams were about dying.

Elena's dreams were about getting old.

Nobody here has not had (will not have) Elena's dreams.

Time is the school in which we learn, / Time is the fire in which we burn: Delmore Schwartz again.

I remember despising the book Dylan Thomas's widow Caitlin wrote after her husband's death, *Leftover Life to Kill*. I remember being dismissive of, even censorious about, her "self-pity," her "whining," her "dwelling on it." *Leftover Life to Kill* was published in 1957. I was twenty-two years old. Time is the school in which we learn.

18.

At the time I began writing these pages, in October 2004, I still did not understand how or why or when John died. I had been there. I had watched while the EMS team tried to bring him back. I still did not know how or why or when. In early December 2004, almost a year after he died, I finally received the autopsy report and emergency room records I had first requested from New York Hospital on the fourteenth of January, two weeks after it happened and one day before I told Quintana that it had happened. One reason it took eleven months to receive these records, I realized when I looked at them, was that I myself had written the wrong address on the hospital's request form. I had at that time lived at the same address on the same street on the Upper East Side of Manhattan for sixteen years. Yet the address I had given the hospital was on another street altogether, where John and I had lived for the five months immediately following our wedding in 1964.

A doctor to whom I mentioned this shrugged, as if I had told him a familiar story.

Either he said that such "cognitive deficits" could be associated with stress or he said that such cognitive deficits could be associated with grief.

It was a mark of those cognitive deficits that within seconds after he said it I had no idea which he had said.

According to the hospital's Emergency Department Nursing Documentation Sheet, the Emergency Medical Services call was received at 9:15 p.m. on the evening of December 30, 2003.

According to the log kept by the doormen the ambulance arrived five minutes later, at 9:20 p.m. During the next forty-five minutes, according to the Nursing Documentation Sheet, the following medications were given, by either direct injection or IV infusion: atropine (times three), epinephrine (times three), vasopressin (40 units), amiodarone (300 mg), high-dose epinephrine (3 mg), and high-dose epinephrine again (5 mg). According to the same documentation the patient was intubated at the scene. I have no memory of an intubation. This may be an error on the part of whoever did the documentation, or it may be another cognitive deficit.

According to the log kept by the doormen the ambulance left for the hospital at 10:05 p.m.

According to the Emergency Department Nursing Documentation Sheet the patient was received for triage at 10:10 p.m. He was described as asystolic and apneic. There was no palpable pulse. There was no pulse via sonography. The mental status was unresponsive. The skin color was pale. The Glasgow Coma Scale rating was 3, the lowest rating possible, indicating that eye, verbal, and motor responses were all absent. Lacerations were seen on the right forehead and the bridge of the nose. Both pupils were fixed and dilated. "Lividity" was noted.

According to the Emergency Department Physician's Record the patient was seen at 10:15 p.m. The physician's notation ended: "Cardiac arrest. DOA—likely massive M.I. Pronounced 10:18 p.m."

According to the Nursing Flow Chart the IV was removed and the patient extubated at 10:20 p.m. At 10:30 p.m. the notation was "wife at bedside—George, soc. worker, at bedside with wife."

According to the autopsy report, examination showed a greater than 95 percent stenosis of both the left main and the left anterior descending arteries. Examination also showed "slight myocardial pallor on TCC staining, indicative of acute infarct in distribution of left anterior descending artery."

I read this paperwork several times. The elapsed time indicated that the time spent at New York Hospital had been, as I had thought, just bookkeeping, hospital procedure, the regularization of a death. Yet each time I read the official sheets I noticed a new detail. On my first reading of the Emergency Department Physician's Record I had not for example registered the letters "DOA." On my first reading of the Emergency Department Physician's Record I was presumably still assimilating the Emergency Department Nursing Documentation Sheet.

"Fixed and dilated" pupils. FDPs.

Sherwin Nuland: "The tenacious young men and women see their patient's pupils become unresponsive to light and then widen until they are large fixed circles of impenetrable blackness. Reluctantly the team stops its efforts. . . . The room is strewn with the debris of the lost campaign . . ."

Fixed circles of impenetrable blackness.

Yes. That was what the ambulance crew saw in John's eyes on our living room floor.

"Lividity." Post-mortem lividity.

I knew what "lividity" meant because it is an issue in morgues. Detectives point it out. It can be a way of deter-

mining time of death. After circulation stops, blood follows the course of gravity, pooling wherever the body is
resting. There is a certain amount of time before this
pooled blood becomes visible to the eye. What I could
not remember was what that amount of time was. I looked
up "lividity" in the handbook on forensic pathology that
John kept on the shelf above his desk. "Although lividity
is variable, it normally begins to form immediately after
death and is usually clearly perceptible within an hour or
two." If lividity was clearly perceptible to the triage
nurses by 10:10 p.m., then, it would have started forming
an hour before.

An hour before was when I was calling the ambulance.

Which meant he was dead then.

*After that instant at the dinner table he was never not
dead.*

I now know how I'm going to die, he had said in 1987
after the left anterior descending artery had been opened
by angioplasty.

*You no more know how you're going to die than I do or
anyone else does,* I had said in 1987.

We call it the widowmaker, pal, his cardiologist in New
York had said about the left anterior descending artery.

Through the summer and fall I had been increasingly fixed on locating the anomaly that could have allowed this to happen.

In my rational mind I knew how it happened. In my rational mind I had spoken to many doctors who told me how it happened. In my rational mind I had read David J. Callans in *The New England Journal of Medicine:* "Although the majority of cases of sudden death from cardiac causes involve patients with preexisting coronary artery disease, cardiac arrest is the first manifestation of this underlying problem in 50 percent of patients. . . . Sudden cardiac arrest is primarily a problem in patients outside of the hospital; in fact, approximately 80 percent of cases of sudden death from cardiac causes occur at home. The rate of success of resuscitation in patients with out-of-hospital cardiac arrest has been poor, averaging 2 to 5 percent in major urban centers. . . . Resuscitation efforts initiated after eight minutes are almost always doomed to fail." In my rational mind I had read Sherwin Nuland in *How We Die:* "When an arrest occurs elsewhere than the hospital, only 20 to 30 percent survive, and these are almost always those who respond quickly to the CPR. If there has been no response by the time of arrival in the emergency room, the likelihood of survival is virtually zero."

In my rational mind I knew that.

I was not however operating from my rational mind.

Had I been operating from my rational mind I would not have been entertaining fantasies that would not have been out of place at an Irish wake. I would not for example have experienced, when I heard that Julia Child had died, so distinct a relief, so marked a sense that *this was finally working out:* John and Julia Child could have dinner together (this had been my immediate thought), she could cook, he could ask her about the OSS, they would amuse each other, like each other. They had once done a breakfast together, in a season when each was promoting a book. She had inscribed a copy of *The Way to Cook* and given it to him.

I found the copy of *The Way to Cook* in the kitchen and looked at the inscription.

"*Bon appetit* to John Gregory Dunne," it read.

Bon appetit to John Gregory Dunne and Julia Child and the OSS.

Nor, had I been operating from my rational mind, would I have given such close attention to "health" stories on the Internet and pharmaceutical advertising on television. I fretted for example over a Bayer commercial for a low-dose aspirin that was said to "significantly reduce" the risk of a heart attack. I knew perfectly well how aspirin reduces the risk of heart attack: it keeps the blood from clotting. I also knew that John was taking Coumadin, a far more powerful anticoagulant. Yet I was seized nonetheless by the possible folly of having overlooked low-dose aspirin. I fretted similarly over a study done by UC–San Diego and Tufts showing a 4.65 percent increase in cardiac death over the fourteen-day period of Christmas and New Year's. I fretted over a study from Vanderbilt demonstrating that erythromycin quintupled the risk of cardiac arrest if taken in conjunction with common heart medications. I fretted over a study on statins, and the 30 to 40 percent jump in the risk of heart attack for patients who stopped taking them.

As I recall this I realize how open we are to the persistent message that we can avert death.

And to its punitive correlative, the message that if death catches us we have only ourselves to blame.

Only after I read the autopsy report did I begin to believe what I had been repeatedly told: nothing he or I had done or not done had either caused or could have prevented his death. He had inherited a bad heart. It would eventually kill him. The date on which it would kill him had already been, by many medical interventions, postponed. When that date did come, no action I could have taken in our living room—no home defibrillator, no CPR, nothing short of a fully equipped crash cart and the technical facility to follow cardioversion within seconds with

IV medication—could have given him even one more day.

The one more day *I love you more than.*

As you used to say to me.

Only after I read the autopsy report did I stop trying to reconstruct the collision, the collapse of the dead star. The collapse had been there all along, invisible, unsuspected.

Greater than 95 percent stenosis of both the left main and the left anterior descending arteries.

Acute infarct in distribution of left anterior descending artery, the LAD.

That was the scenario. The LAD got fixed in 1987 and it stayed fixed until everybody forgot about it and then it got unfixed. *We call it the widowmaker, pal,* the cardiologist had said in 1987.

I tell you that I shall not live two days, Gawain said.

When something happens to me, John had said.

19.

I have trouble thinking of myself as a widow. I remember hesitating the first time I had to check that box on the "marital status" part of a form. I also had trouble thinking of myself as a wife. Given the value I placed on the rituals of domestic life, the concept of "wife" should not have seemed difficult, but it did. For a long time after we were married I had trouble with the ring. It was loose enough to slip off my left ring finger, so for a year or two I wore it on my right. After I burned the right finger taking a pan from the oven, I put the ring on a gold chain around my neck. When Quintana was born and someone gave her a baby ring I added her ring to the chain.

This seemed to work.

I still wear the rings that way.

"You want a different kind of wife," I frequently said to John in the first years of our marriage. I usually said this on the way back to Portuguese Bend after dinner in town.

It was typically the initial volley in those fights that started as we passed the refineries off the San Diego Freeway. "You should have married someone more like Lenny." Lenny was my sister-in-law, Nick's wife. Lenny entertained and had lunch with friends and ran her house effortlessly and wore beautiful French dresses and suits and was always available to look at a house or give a baby shower or take visitors from out of town to Disneyland. "If I wanted to marry someone more like Lenny I would have married someone more like Lenny," John would say, at first patiently, then less so.

In fact I had no idea how to be a wife.

In those first years I would pin daisies in my hair, trying for a "bride" effect.

Later I had matching gingham skirts made for me and Quintana, trying for "young mother."

My memory of those years is that both John and I were improvising, flying blind. When I was clearing out a file drawer recently I came across a thick file labeled "Planning." The very fact that we made files labeled "Planning" suggests how little of it we did. We also had "planning meetings," which consisted of sitting down with legal pads, stating the day's problem out loud, and then, with no further attempt to solve it, going out to lunch. Such lunches were festive, as if to celebrate a job well done. Michael's, in Santa Monica, was a typical venue. In this particular "Planning" file I found

several Christmas lists from the 1970s, a few notes on
telephone calls, and, the bulk of the file, many notes,
again dating from the 1970s, having to do with projected
expenses and income. A mood of desperation permeates
these notes. There was a note made for a meeting with Gil
Frank on April 19, 1978, when we were trying to sell the
house in Malibu to pay for the house in Brentwood Park
on which we had already put down a $50,000 deposit. We
could not sell the house in Malibu because it rained all
that spring. Slopes fell. The Pacific Coast Highway was
closed. No one could even look at the house unless they
already lived on the Malibu side of the washout. Over a
period of some weeks we had only one viewer, a psychiatrist who lived in the Malibu Colony. He left his shoes
outside in the driving rain to "get the feel of the house,"
walked around barefoot on the tile floor, and reported to
his son, who reported to Quintana, that the house was
"cold." This was the note made on April 19 of that year:
*We must assume we will not sell Malibu until end of year.
We have to assume the worst so that any improvement will
seem better.*

A note made a week later, I can only think for a "planning meeting": *Discuss: Abandon Brentwood Park? Eat
the $50,000?*

Two weeks later we flew to Honolulu, thinking to escape the rain and sort out our dwindling options. The
next morning when we came in from swimming there was

a message: the sun had come out in Malibu and we had an offer within range of the asking.

What had encouraged us to think that a resort hotel in Honolulu was the place to solve a cash shortfall?

What lesson did we take from the fact that it worked?

Twenty-five years later, confronted with a similar shortfall and similarly deciding to sort it out in Paris, how could we have seen it as economizing because we got one ticket free on the Concorde?

In the same file drawer I found a few paragraphs John had written in 1990, on our twenty-sixth anniversary. "She wore sunglasses throughout the service the day we got married, at the little mission church in San Juan Bautista, California; she also wept through the entire ceremony. As we walked down the aisle, we promised each other that we could get out of this next week and not wait until death did us part."

That worked too. Somehow it had all worked.

Why did I think that this improvisation could never end?

If I had seen that it could, what would I have done differently?

What would he?

20.

I am writing now as the end of the first year approaches. The sky in New York is dark when I wake at seven and darkening again by four in the afternoon. There are colored Christmas lights on the quince branches in the living room. There were also colored Christmas lights on quince branches in the living room a year ago, on the night it happened, but in the spring, not long after I brought Quintana home from UCLA, those strings burned out, went dead. This served as a symbol. I bought new strings of colored lights. This served as a profession of faith in the future. I take the opportunity for such professions where and when I can invent them, since I do not yet actually feel this faith in the future.

I notice that I have lost the skills for ordinary social encounters, however undeveloped those skills may have been, that I had a year ago. During the Republican convention I was invited to a small party at a friend's apartment. I was happy to see the friend and I was happy to see her father, who was the reason for the party, but I found conversation with others difficult. I noticed as I was leaving that the Secret Service was there but lacked even the patience to stay long enough to learn what important person was coming. On another evening during the Republican convention I went to a party given by *The New York Times* in the Time Warner building. There were candles and gardenias floating in glass cubes. I could not focus on whoever I was talking to. I was focused only on the gardenias getting sucked into the filter at the house in Brentwood Park.

On such occasions I hear myself trying to make an effort and failing.

I notice that I get up from dinner too abruptly.

I also notice that I do not have the resilience I had a year ago. A certain number of crises occur and the mechanism that floods the situation with adrenaline burns out. Mobilization becomes unreliable, slow or absent. In August and September, after the Democratic and Republican conventions but before the election, I wrote, for the first time since John died, a piece. It was about the campaign. It was the first piece I had written since 1963 that he did not read in draft form and tell me what was wrong, what was needed, how to bring it up here, take it down there. I have never written pieces fluently but this one seemed to be taking even longer than usual: I realized at some point that I was unwilling to finish it, because there was no one to read it. I kept telling myself that I had a deadline, that John and I never missed deadlines. Whatever I finally did to finish this piece was as close as I have ever come to imagining a message from him. The message was simple: *You're a professional. Finish the piece.*

It occurs to me that we allow ourselves to imagine only such messages as we need to survive.

The trach at UCLA, I recognize now, was going to happen with or without me.

Quintana resuming her life, I recognize now, was going to happen with or without me.

Finishing this piece, which was to say resuming my own life, was not.

When I checked the piece for publication I was startled and unsettled by how many mistakes I had made: simple errors of transcription, names and dates wrong. I told myself that this was temporary, part of the mobilization problem, further evidence of those cognitive deficits that came with either stress or grief, but I remained unsettled. Would I ever be right again? Could I ever again trust myself not to be wrong?

Do you always have to be right? He had said that.

Is it impossible for you to consider the possibility that you might be wrong?

Increasingly I find myself focusing on the similarities between these December days and the same December days a year ago. In certain ways those similar days a year ago have more clarity for me, a sharper focus. I do many of the same things. I make the same lists of things undone. I wrap Christmas presents in the same colored tissue, write the same messages on the same postcards from the Whitney gift shop, affix the postcards to the colored tissue with the same gold notary seals. I write the same checks for the building staff, except the checks are now imprinted with only my name. I would not have changed the checks (any more than I would change the voice on the answering machine) but it was said to be essential that John's name now appear only on trust accounts. I order the same kind of ham from Citarella. I fret the same way over the number of plates I will need on Christmas Eve, count and recount. I keep an annual December dentist's appointment and realize as I am putting the sample toothbrushes into my bag that no one will be waiting for me in the reception room, reading the papers until we can go to breakfast at 3 Guys on Madison Avenue. The morning goes empty. When I pass 3 Guys I look the other way. A friend asks me to go with her to hear the Christmas music at St. Ignatius Loyola, and we walk home in the dark in the rain. That night the first snow falls, although only a dusting, no avalanching off the roof of St. James', nothing like my birthday a year ago.

My birthday a year ago when he gave me the last present he would ever give me.

My birthday a year ago when he had twenty-five nights left to live.

On the table in front of the fireplace I notice something out of place in the stack of books nearest the chair in which John sat to read when he woke in the middle of the night. I have deliberately left this stack untouched, not from any shrine-building impulse but because I did not believe that I could afford to think about what he read in the middle of the night. Now someone has placed on top of the stack, balanced precariously, a large illustrated coffee-table book, *The Agnelli Gardens at Villar Perosa.* I move *The Agnelli Gardens at Villar Perosa.* Beneath it is a heavily marked copy of John Lukacs's *Five Days in London: May 1940,* in which there is a laminated bookmark that reads, in a child's handwriting, *John—happy reading to you—from John, age 7.* I am at first puzzled by the bookmark, which under the lamination is dusted with festive pink glitter, then remember: the Creative Artists Agency, as a Christmas project every year, "adopts" a group of Los Angeles schoolchildren, each of whom in turn makes a keepsake for a designated CAA client.

He would have opened the box from CAA on Christmas night.

He would have stuck the bookmark in whatever book was on top of that stack.

He would have had one hundred and twenty hours left to live.

How would he have chosen to live those one hundred and twenty hours?

Beneath the copy of *Five Days in London* is a copy of *The New Yorker* dated January 5, 2004. A copy of *The New Yorker* with that issue date would have been delivered to our apartment on Sunday, December 28, 2003. On Sunday, December 28, 2003, according to John's calendar, we had dinner at home with Sharon DeLano, who had been his editor at Random House and was at that time his editor at *The New Yorker*. We would have had dinner at the table in the living room. According to my kitchen notebook we ate linguine Bolognese and a salad and cheese and a baguette. At that point he would have had forty-eight hours left to live.

Some premonition of this timetable was why I had not touched the stack of books in the first place.

I don't think I'm up for this, he had said in the taxi on our way down from Beth Israel North that night or the next night. He was talking about the condition in which we had once again left Quintana.

You don't get a choice, I had said in the taxi.

I have wondered since if he did.

21.

S he's still beautiful," Gerry had said as he and John and I left Quintana in the ICU at Beth Israel North.

"He said she's still beautiful," John said in the taxi. "Did you hear him say that? She's still beautiful? She's lying there swollen up with tubes coming out of her and he said—"

He could not continue.

That happened on one of those late December nights a few days before he died. Whether it happened on the 26th or the 27th or the 28th or the 29th I have no idea. It did not happen on the 30th because Gerry had already left the hospital by the time we got there on the 30th. I realize that much of my energy during the past months has been given to counting back the days, the hours. At the moment he was saying in the taxi on the way down from Beth Israel North that everything he had done was worthless did he have three hours left to live or did he have twenty-seven? Did he know how few hours there were, did he feel himself going, was he saying that he did not want to leave? *Don't let the Broken Man catch me,* Quintana would say when she woke from bad dreams, one of the "sayings" John put in the box and borrowed for Cat in *Dutch Shea, Jr.* I had promised her that we would not let the Broken Man catch her.

You're safe.

I'm here.

I had believed that we had that power.

Now the Broken Man was in the ICU at Beth Israel North waiting for her and now the Broken Man was in this taxi waiting for her father. Even at three or four she had recognized that when it came to the Broken Man she could rely only on her own efforts: *If the Broken Man comes I'll hang onto the fence and won't let him take me.*

She hung onto the fence. Her father did not.

I tell you I shall not live two days.

What gives those December days a year ago their sharper focus is their ending.

22.

As the grandchild of a geologist I learned early to
anticipate the absolute mutability of hills and water-
falls and even islands. When a hill slumps into the
ocean I see the order in it. When a 5.2 on the
Richter Scale wrenches the writing table in my own
room in my own house in my own particular
Welbeck Street I keep on typing. A hill is a transi-
tional accommodation to stress, and ego may be
a similar accommodation. A waterfall is a self-
correcting maladjustment of stream to structure,
and so, for all I know, is technique. The very island
to which Inez Victor returned in the spring of
1975—Oahu, an emergent post-erosional land mass
along the Hawaiian Ridge—is a temporary feature,
and every rainfall or tremor along the Pacific plates
alters its shape and shortens its tenure as Cross-
roads of the Pacific. In this light it is difficult to

maintain definite convictions about what happened down there in the spring of 1975, or before.

This passage is from the beginning of a novel I wrote during the early 1980s, *Democracy*. John named it. I had begun it as a comedy of family manners with the title *Angel Visits*, a phrase defined by *Brewer's Dictionary of Phrase and Fable* as "delightful intercourse of short duration and rare occurrence," but when it became clear that it was going in a different direction I had kept writing without a title. When I finished John read it and said I should call it *Democracy*. I looked up the passage after the 9.0 Richter earthquake along a six-hundred-mile section of the Sumatran subduction zone had triggered the tsunami that wiped out large parts of coastline bordering the Indian Ocean.

I am unable to stop trying to imagine this event.

There is no video of what I try to imagine. There are no beaches, no flooded swimming pools, no hotel lobbies breaking up like rotted pilings in a storm. What I want to see happened under the surface. The India Plate buckling as it thrust under the Burma Plate. The current sweeping unseen through the deep water. I do not have a depth chart for the Indian Ocean but can pick up the broad outline even from my Rand McNally cardboard globe. Seven hundred and eighty meters off Banda Aceh. Twenty-three hundred between Sumatra and Sri Lanka.

Twenty-one hundred between the Andamans and Thailand and then a long shallowing toward Phuket. The instant when the leading edge of the unseen current got slowed by the continental shelf. The buildup of water as the bottom of the shelf began to shallow out.

As it was in the beginning, is now and ever shall be, world without end.

It is now December 31, 2004, a year and a day.

On December 24, Christmas Eve, I had people for dinner, just as John and I had done on Christmas Eve a year before. I told myself that I was doing this for Quintana but I was also doing it for myself, a pledge that I would not lead the rest of my life as a special case, a guest, someone who could not function on her own. I built a fire, I lit candles, I laid out plates and silver on a buffet table in the dining room. I put out some CDs, Mabel Mercer singing Cole Porter and Israel Kamakawiwo'ole singing "Over the Rainbow" and an Israeli jazz pianist named Liz Magnes playing "Someone to Watch Over Me." John had been seated next to Liz Magnes once at a dinner at the Israeli mission and she had sent him the CD, a Gershwin concert she had given in Marrakech. In its ability to suggest drinks at the King David Hotel in Jerusalem during the British period this CD had seemed to John spectrally interesting, recovered evidence of a vanished world, one more reverberation from World War One. He referred to it as "the Mandate music." He had put it on while he was reading before dinner the night he died.

About five in the afternoon on the 24th I thought I could not do the evening but when the time came the evening did itself.

Susanna Moore sent leis from Honolulu for her daughter Lulu and Quintana and me. We wore the leis. Another friend brought a gingerbread house. There were many children. I played the Mandate music, although the noise level was such that no one heard it.

On Christmas morning I put away the plates and silver and in the afternoon I went up to St. John the Divine, where there were mainly Japanese tourists. There were always Japanese tourists at St. John the Divine. On the afternoon Quintana got married at St. John the Divine there had been Japanese tourists snapping pictures as she and Gerry left the altar. On the afternoon we placed John's ashes in the chapel off the main altar at St. John the Divine an empty Japanese tour bus had caught fire and burned outside, a pillar of flame on Amsterdam Avenue. On Christmas Day the chapel off the main altar was blocked off, part of the cathedral reconstruction. A security guard took me in. The chapel was emptied, filled only with scaffolding. I ducked under the scaffolding and found the marble plate with John's name and my mother's name. I hung the lei from one of the brass rods that held the marble plate to the vault and then I walked from the chapel back into the nave and out the main aisle, straight toward the big rose window.

As I walked I kept my eyes on the window, half blinded by its brilliance but determined to keep my gaze fixed until I caught the moment in which the window as approached seems to explode with light, fill the entire field of vision with blue. The Christmas of the Buffalo pens and the black wafer alarm clock and the neighborhood fireworks all over Honolulu, the Christmas of 1990, the Christmas during which John and I had been doing the crash rewrite on the picture that never got made, had involved that window. We had staged the denouement of the picture at St. John the Divine, placed a plutonium device in the bell tower (only the protagonist realizes that the device is at St. John the Divine and not the World Trade towers), blown the unwitting carrier of the device straight out through the big rose window. We had filled the screen with blue that Christmas.

I realize as I write this that I do not want to finish this account.

Nor did I want to finish the year.

The craziness is receding but no clarity is taking its place.

I look for resolution and find none.

I did not want to finish the year because I know that as the days pass, as January becomes February and February becomes summer, certain things will happen. My image of John at the instant of his death will become less immediate, less raw. It will become something that happened in another year. My sense of John himself, John alive, will become more remote, even "mudgy," softened, transmuted into whatever best serves my life without him. In fact this is already beginning to happen. All year I have been keeping time by last year's calendar: what were we doing on this day last year, where did we have dinner, is it the day a year ago we flew to Honolulu after Quintana's wedding, is it the day a year ago we flew back from Paris, *is it the day.* I realized today for the first time that my memory of this day a year ago is a memory that does not involve John. This day a year ago was December 31, 2003. John did not see this day a year ago. John was dead.

I was crossing Lexington Avenue when this occurred to me.

I know why we try to keep the dead alive: we try to keep them alive in order to keep them with us.

I also know that if we are to live ourselves there comes

a point at which we must relinquish the dead, let them go, keep them dead.

Let them become the photograph on the table.

Let them become the name on the trust accounts.

Let go of them in the water.

Knowing this does not make it any easier to let go of him in the water.

In fact the apprehension that our life together will decreasingly be the center of my every day seemed today on Lexington Avenue so distinct a betrayal that I lost all sense of oncoming traffic.

I think about leaving the lei at St. John the Divine.

A souvenir of the Christmas in Honolulu when we filled the screen with blue.

During the years when people still left Honolulu on the Matson Lines the custom at the moment of departure was to throw leis on the water, a promise that the traveler would return. The leis would get caught in the wake and go bruised and brown, the way the gardenias in the pool filter at the house in Brentwood Park had gone bruised and brown.

The other morning when I woke I tried to remember the arrangement of the rooms in the house in Brentwood Park. I imagined myself walking through the rooms, first on the ground floor and then on the second. Later in the day I realized that I had forgotten one.

The lei I left at St. John the Divine would have gone brown by now.

Leis go brown, tectonic plates shift, deep currents move, islands vanish, rooms get forgotten.

I flew into Indonesia and Malaysia and Singapore with John, in 1979 and 1980.

Some of the islands that were there then would now be gone, just shallows.

I think about swimming with him into the cave at Portuguese Bend, about the swell of clear water, the way it changed, the swiftness and power it gained as it narrowed through the rocks at the base of the point. The tide had to be just right. We had to be in the water at the very moment the tide was right. We could only have done this a half dozen times at most during the two years we lived there but it is what I remember. Each time we did it I was afraid of missing the swell, hanging back, timing it wrong. John never was. You had to feel the swell change. You had to go with the change. He told me that. No eye is on the sparrow but he did tell me that.

A NOTE ON THE TYPE

This book was set in Bodoni, a typeface named after Giambattista Bodoni (1740-1813), the celebrated printer and type designer of Parma. The Bodoni types of today were designed not as faithful reproductions of any one of the Bodoni fonts but rather as a composite, modern version of the Bodoni manner. Bodoni's innovations in type style included a greater degree of contrast in the thick and thin elements of the letters and a sharper and more angular finish of details.